# Gaza Medic

Other books by Richard Villar include:

*Knife Edge – Life as a Special Forces Surgeon* (Vineyard Press)

*Winged Scalpel – Surgeon at the Frontline of Disaster*
(Pen & Sword Military)

*Never a Straight Line – Travels Through Chile and Bolivia*
(Vineyard Press)

*An Englishman Goes Walking – Through the Alps to the Sea*
(Vineyard Press)

# Pre-publication Reviews

*Lt Col (Retd) Richard Williams MBE MC, former Commanding Officer 22 SAS*
Read this book if you want to learn how to keep your head whilst saving lives in one of the most dangerous war zones in the world today.

*Ayesha Sheereen, Student of Comparative Literature and Russian (University of St Andrews, United Kingdom)*
There are no words. In a couple of sittings, I devoured *Gaza Medic* and now there are tears running down my face. What Richard Villar has written is one of the most powerful pieces of prose I've read in a long time. The most important book I've ever had the privilege of reading, perhaps. It was raw, honest, vulnerable, humane, captivating and incredibly written.

*Major General A P N Currie CB CBE (Winchester, United Kingdom)*
This is an extremely compelling book, one which anybody seeking to understand the realities of the war in Gaza should read… In places it might well make you weep, particularly for the children. It will also – or it should – make you angry.

*Chris Coe, Photographer, Founder & Director of Travel Photographer of the Year and Chair of the British Guild of Travel Writers (Suffolk, United Kingdom)*
In Gaza there are only losers… Read *Gaza Medic*, even if you think you know what is happening. Read it regardless of your political or religious allegiances… It's a wakeup call to the world and our so called leaders.

*Enrique Steiger MD, Founder SWISSCROSS.ORG (Zurich, Switzerland)*
This book is more than just a memoir or a war diary; it is a testament to resilience and humanity amidst unimaginable atrocities… Let us focus on what unites us rather than what divides us and work tirelessly to create a world where future generations inherit peace and prosperity.

*Vincent K. Solomon MS FICS FACS (Mungeli, India)*
Villar exemplified raw courage in the midst of chaos and his book is a revelation affirming that any kind of war, logical or illogical, religious or political needs to be shunned and condemned.

*Sylvie Thoral (Marseille, France)*
I had pleasure in reading this book… a great merit is to explain the challenges and specifics of war surgery to non-medics… the ecological damage of warfare… Palestinian society… a conflict that is one of the most extensively analysed and yet polarisation is still at its peak… testimonies like Richard Villar's remain as important as ever…

*Alain Tranchemontagne, CEO HydroCision (Rhode Island, USA)*
Visceral. The raw reality is eye opening. A must read to grasp ground-level nuances of one of the most important challenges of the century!

*Col (retd) David Vassallo FRCSEd DHMSA MA (History of Warfare) L/RAMC, Chairman, Friends of Millbank, UK (www.friendsofmillbank.org)*
If you could choose only one book to visualise and appreciate the tragic reality of Gaza at war, and frontline surgery, this is the book. Be inspired, and in your own way bring some light into the Gaza darkness.

*RJL, UKSF(R)/Security Consultant/Oil and Gas Engineer (Newmarket, United Kingdom)*
*Gaza Medic* is a must-read for anyone who wants to understand what it is like to operate in a warzone where chaos rules, and civilian suffering is at the heart of the conflict.

*Dr Stephen Cumbers MB BS MSc MRCGP MRSC CSci FIBMS FRSA, Medical Doctor and Chartered Scientist (London, United Kingdom)*
…a powerful and inspirational first-hand account of practical humanity in the face of raw inhumanity.

*Tony Williams, Proof-reader (Beverley, United Kingdom)*
Extremely well written and tells the horrors of the Gaza War bravely and without pulling any punches.

These reviews are extracts. Their full wording can be found on the publisher's website by scanning the following QR code:

# Gaza Medic

## A War Surgeon's Story 2024

Richard Villar

Pen & Sword
**MILITARY**

First published in Great Britain in 2024 by
Pen & Sword Military
An imprint of Pen & Sword Books Limited
Yorkshire – Philadelphia

Copyright © Richard Villar 2024

ISBN 978 1 03615 020 4

The right of Richard Villar to be identified as
Author of this Work has been asserted by him in accordance
with the Copyright, Designs and Patents Act 1988.

A CIP catalogue record for this book is
available from the British Library

All rights reserved. No part of this book may be reproduced or transmitted in any form or by any means, electronic or mechanical including photocopying, recording or by any information storage and retrieval system, without permission from the Publisher in writing.

Typeset by Mac Style
Printed in the UK by CPI Group (UK) Ltd, Croydon, CR0 4YY.

Pen & Sword Books Limited incorporates the imprints of After the Battle, Atlas, Archaeology, Aviation, Discovery, Family History, Fiction, History, Maritime, Military, Military Classics, Politics, Select, Transport, True Crime, Air World, Frontline Publishing, Leo Cooper, Remember When, Seaforth Publishing, The Praetorian Press, Wharncliffe Local History, Wharncliffe Transport, Wharncliffe True Crime and White Owl.

For a complete list of Pen & Sword titles please contact

PEN & SWORD BOOKS LIMITED
47 Church Street, Barnsley, South Yorkshire, S70 2AS, England
E-mail: enquiries@pen-and-sword.co.uk
Website: www.pen-and-sword.co.uk
or
PEN AND SWORD BOOKS
1950 Lawrence Road, Havertown, PA 19083, USA
E-mail: uspen-and-sword@casematepublishers.com
Website: www.penandswordbooks.com

*To those affected by warfare, wherever you may be.
You deserve better.*

# Contents

*Foreword* — xi

| | | |
|---|---|---|
| **Chapter 1** | Getting Ready for Gaza | 1 |
| **Chapter 2** | The Team Assembles | 11 |
| **Chapter 3** | My Name is Abu Ruairidh | 19 |
| **Chapter 4** | The Human Shield in Arish | 27 |
| **Chapter 5** | Into Gaza | 37 |
| **Chapter 6** | Arriving at Al Aqsa | 47 |
| **Chapter 7** | When Palestinians Worry | 61 |
| **Chapter 8** | A Stoical Civilisation | 73 |
| **Chapter 9** | War is About People | 83 |
| **Chapter 10** | Huge Wounds and Mental Health | 95 |
| **Chapter 11** | One Million Operations | 105 |
| **Chapter 12** | This Illogical War | 115 |
| **Chapter 13** | Gaza Could Be So Beautiful | 127 |
| **Chapter 14** | The True Leader | 137 |
| **Chapter 15** | Patch, Mend, and Save | 147 |
| **Chapter 16** | Spreading the Message | 157 |
| **Chapter 17** | Leaving Gaza | 167 |

*Acknowledgements* — 171

# Map of Gaza

# Foreword

**W**hat am I doing here? Unless I think hard, it is difficult to explain, as most would see me as crazy.

It is 2:30 in the morning in Central Gaza and I am lying on a wafer-thin mattress on a chipped tile floor. I am in a side room of an overcrowded hospital ward. The administration has turned this into accommodation, although can ill afford to lose the space for patient care. Around me are four colleagues, each on their own wafer-thin mattress. One is snoring contentedly, the others are breathing quietly. I am busy listening.

It is dark both indoors and out, while high in the sky above us, beyond the ajar tilt window to our room, flies an Israeli surveillance drone. It makes a noise like a huge mosquito. The locals call it a *zinnanah*, a name that has stuck in my mind, even for my British tongue. I am generally hopeless at speaking Arabic. Ambulance sirens are constant, as are the horns of cars, or the braying of donkeys in a hurry. Whatever transport is used to bring a casualty to my hospital, the dead and wounded are the same – almost always women, children, and the elderly, with the occasional younger male. Each has the multiple injuries that shells and missiles create. Single bullets tend to cause single injuries, but shells and missiles are different.

Occasionally I hear the rat-ta-tat-tat of a heavy machine gun as a tank, perhaps an Apache helicopter, has a go at its next target, although the logic of its target acquisition escapes me. It is said that Artificial Intelligence is being used for this but as with all computers, rubbish in is rubbish out. When it comes to human life, I cannot see the advantage of blaming a computer. There are crumps and thumps, too, as shells and missiles hit something solid. The shredded curtains across our window billow each time there is an explosion, while the fragmentation film stuck to the pane has so far prevented the glass from shattering. Shattered glass is dangerous, and can make me a casualty as well, so I stay below the level of the windowsill, just in case. The fighting is not far away.

It is 2024, Deir-al-Balah in Central Gaza, and I have been inserted amid a social media blackout, as part of an Emergency Medical Team for a humanitarian organisation. I am an orthopaedic surgeon, that is bones and joints, and have been to plenty of war zones and natural disasters. We are there to support the dwindling local Palestinian staff. They are being decimated, most are unpaid, many have been killed, while others have fled to somewhere they consider safer. Yet there is no safe place in Gaza. This is a free-fire zone, as evidenced by the seven aid workers from World Central Kitchen who were killed 24 hours ago. Many organisations withdrew at that moment but mine did not. We went forward when others went back.

It is the way of things with humanitarian war surgery, and this is the war to beat many. The Palestinians are dropping like flies. I hear the casualties screaming outside our door, the orphaned children crying, the widowed mothers wailing, the fathers cursing, and I realise that soon we must be active in the operating theatre. There is a mass casualty incident underway, such things are daily in 2024 Gaza, and there are lives to save, arteries to tie, fractures to fix, wounds to explore, shrapnel to remove, and blood, if any, to transfuse. The paramedics have done what they can *en route* to the hospital, but now it is our turn. The Palestinians are a mighty people, astonishingly strong, a civilisation under threat, but six months into this unreasonable, one-sided, illogical war, even they are cracking. It is time to act.

Why me? I have no reason, other than to sit idly by is the same as being complicit. My family, friends, children, and grandchildren need to know that I did something positive, and I brought some light into the Gaza darkness. Talking, taking sides, or having an opinion is insufficient. My home is in the UK, where I heard the regular news bulletins and realised that my government was trying to steer public opinion. I am a surgeon, not a politician, and I do not take sides. I have one focus only, the patient on the stretcher, bed, mattress, or floor before me. If I act quickly, if each member of my team does the same, another life saved is our achievement.

It is time to get up and start work…

\* \* \*

What follows is a true story based on the diary I kept as a war surgeon at a Palestinian hospital in Central Gaza during the Israeli invasion after the Hamas attacks of 7 October 2023. It was a time when the Israeli troops were advancing, and fellow humans were dropping around me. At the end of each long day, at a time when day went into night and back to day again, I sat down to write. I read my words now and instantly feel uncomfortable, a gnawing in my stomach's pit, sweat on my forehead, a racing pulse, a near imperceptible tremor in my fingers, and dilated pupils.

Writing these words was difficult. When I was in Gaza, I must have developed a shell to protect me from the full horror, but without realising it. Yet now, as I look back, I am troubled. It will take me a very long time to recover from my Gaza experience; indeed, perhaps I will never achieve that. All I can hope is that my efforts, our efforts, were worthwhile.

\* \* \*

## Chapter 1

# Getting Ready for Gaza

Another day, another year, another conflict. This time it was Gaza. I could not explain why I was involved at all, yet I was. Perhaps it was because I had done this many times before and others saw me as experienced. That may have been true, but I was still terrified, confused and puzzled although I dared not show my emotions to anyone. Outwardly, I had to appear in control.

I was scheduled to leave for Gaza in 72 hours with an organisation called Medical Aid for Palestinians (MAP). My mobile was alive with messages coming at me from all angles – family, friends, and colleagues I had yet to meet. MAP had been running Emergency Medical Teams

(EMTs) in support of the latest Gaza conflict for the previous three months and I was scheduled to form part of their fifth team, EMT5. I was originally going to join EMT2 nearly three months earlier but somehow fell off a Lake District mountain and dislocated my left shoulder. Two days later, with me guzzling codeine and the occasional whisky for pain, MAP's invitation arrived. I could not accept when I had one arm in a sling. But three months later, after near-continuous rehabilitation, my shoulder was fine and ready to do whatever was needed. I was almost back to normal.

The news from Gaza was not good. I had been glued to the radio and television each day since the war had begun, in the wake of a Hamas attack on Israel on 7 October 2023. Now that I knew I was going, I was listening to the bulletins less often. I needed no reminding of the dangers that lay ahead. Perhaps it was a form of coping. Shells and missiles were falling, apartment blocks crumbling, and casualties were mounting. I did not believe the official figures. To me, for every death in war there should be up to ten injured. The figures from Gaza suggested only two injured for every death. I wagered to myself, when this conflict was over, and all wars finish eventually, the injured would be many times more than suggested.

To enter Gaza, I would be using the southerly Rafah crossing, on Gaza's frontier with Egypt, and assuming it was open. The crossing was at the edge of the city of Rafah, Gaza's most southerly population centre. Before the war, Rafah had a population of approximately 170,000. Thanks to the forced displacement of Gaza's Palestinians from elsewhere in the territory, this had risen to at least 1.4 million. These were called Internally Displaced Persons (IDPs) and were not officially refugees, even if that is what they were.

Israel continued to make a noise about its forthcoming attack on Rafah. That would be a problem, not only for the huge numbers of casualties such an attack would generate, but I wagered that if Rafah was attacked the crossing would be closed. Although up to 35,000 people crossed each month, it closed quite commonly. For example, after the capture of Israeli soldier Gilad Shalit by Hamas in 2006, the crossing was closed 76 per cent of the time. After Hamas' takeover of Gaza the following year, it was closed permanently, except for infrequent openings by Egypt. If I was outside Gaza, and the Rafah crossing was closed, I would be unable to get in. If I was inside Gaza, and the crossing was closed, I would be unable to get out. Neither option was appealing.

At that moment, Israel's efforts were in the north of Gaza, focussed on the area of Gaza City's Al Shifa Hospital. Israel claimed there were Hamas command centres in the vicinity. That was news to me, as I had previously worked in Al Shifa Hospital and never once saw anything related to Hamas activity, while I had the freedom to roam wherever I wished. Doubtless the blaming would continue, and I should let it do so, however frustrated I might feel. I had zero political view, which was the advantage of being a doctor, as my focus remained solely on the injured, irrespective of from where they had come.

I last visited Gaza in 2018 during the Great March of Return (GMR). This was when many Palestinians tried to cross the border fence into Israel but were shot by Israeli forces in the process. I was the surgeon on the spot, working for the International Committee of the Red Cross (ICRC) in a hospital in the Gaza city of Khan Yunis. I saw many hundreds of injured, plus plenty of dead. Many of the injured had received a single high-velocity gunshot wound to one or other shinbone (tibia), and it was evident that the intention had been to wound rather than kill. It meant my own workload increased exponentially, as injuries are what I do. Deaths, although tragic, did not end up with the surgeon but the wounded certainly did.

The repeated single-shot lower limb injuries meant that I spent a long time and multiple operations over several weeks or months before managing to control a casualty's injuries. Even then, the victim's life was ruined. All I could do was improve things, maybe save a life, but a full cure was largely impossible. For the casualty, there would be no job, no marriage, no children, ongoing poverty, and a reliance on whatever aid might be available from outside Gaza.

The apparent policy of wounding, not killing, had prevented a large percentage of the Gaza population from doing anything worthwhile thereafter. Whatever I did, however skilled I might have been seen by others, it was not feasible to convert an injured victim back to normal. All I could do was stabilise and control. Postoperative complications were usual, not rarities, as might be seen in more peaceful surroundings, and infection was the rule not the exception. Back home in the UK, I work on an infection rate of 0.25 per cent of my patients. Even that small percentage distresses me. After the GMR, an infection rate of 80 per cent was normal. The contrast between the UK and Gaza was huge.

I often worry about my own mental health, not only that of my patients. I well remember Friday 30 March 2018, the first day of the GMR, when I was in Khan Yunis. The GMR continued largely weekly until the end of 2019. That first day, 30 March 2018, the casualties were arriving in huge numbers – one became two, two became four, then eight, 16, 32, 64, 128, 256, and upward. I was in the operating theatre complex, immersed in the chaos of conflict, and suddenly I felt overwhelmed. No specific event triggered the feeling, it seemed simply to happen. It had all become too much.

I was witnessing injuries of unarmed people by others with modern, high-velocity weapons. Those who were armed, people I had never met, appeared to enjoy what they were doing although doubtless they would claim to be following orders. Both shooters and victims were about the same age, had families, loves, ambitions, hopes, mobile telephones, email addresses, social media accounts, and plenty more. Both sides of the conflict might as well have come from the same family. One was poor, the other more fortunate, but as human beings were identical.

That day, as the injured kept coming, I became increasingly exhausted, so took shelter in a small room called the sluice. There is a sluice in most theatre complexes. It is where dirty things are done, bedpans emptied, contaminated dressings discarded, and pus-filled dressings thrown away. The sluice is infrequently used so was where I took shelter, surrounded by the detritus of conflict. I wanted to be alone. I sighed, took in lungfuls of contaminated air, shed several tears, and somehow regathered my emotions. Fifteen minutes later I was back at work, and no one had seen my disappearance. Yet my emotional response had been clear.

I may be a medic and must erect some form of protective shell around me, but I carry the same emotions as anyone. To witness so much injury to otherwise healthy individuals was difficult. I try to bottle things up and hide them from view, but they are bubbling away just beneath the surface. It does not take much for them to re-emerge.

My worry about returning to Gaza after Hamas' October 2023 attack was that my protective shell might once again be breached. I had to go, felt committed, yet was wary about the effect of returning to the medical frontline of conflict. Old hands like me do have feelings.

Perhaps to avoid thinking about the imminent dangers, I kept myself busy, so had a haircut.

"I need it tidied but do not wish to look like a soldier", I instructed a London barber. I did not say why but I am sure he guessed, as he originated from Syria's Damascus and was more than familiar with conflict.

"Leave it to me," he replied. He likely realised I might soon be at the far end of a telescopic sight, and I needed to dissuade a sniper from squeezing their trigger. A non-military haircut was partly my solution.

I had decided to keep my visit to Gaza under wraps. There was no purpose in telling the world of my plans, especially as Gaza was open house on aid workers at that time. At least 200 had already been killed. I decided to say that I was going walking in the French Alps, as that would allow me to disappear without anyone being suspicious. I was a mountain walker anyway. That said, I was unsure if anyone would believe me as my family and friends knew what I was like, so for me to appear in Gaza might for them be unsurprising. Despite the fib, it made sense to only tell a small number of people what I truly intended. I could say more once it was over.

I also made a short video, which I had left in a secret location. It was barely two minutes long and I filmed it in a remote location overlooking the Lake District's Windermere. Alongside the video was the instruction that it should only be released if I failed to make it home. Looking at news bulletins, there were significant dangers ahead and I could only minimise, not avoid them. Only a few weeks before, the accommodation used by an earlier EMT was bombed, fortunately without any deaths, although there were certainly injuries. None of the explanations about why the bombing occurred was persuasive but then I believed almost nothing in war.

Gaza had also sent a long list of the equipment it needed, although why it had delivered the list so late in the day puzzled me. There were many basics such as surgical gowns and gloves, simple dressings, and everyday medicines that might be routine in London but were impossible to find in Gaza. I had also been asked to find some operating loupes. These were fancy glasses that a surgeon could wear when operating. Loupes help magnify the tissues, for example they can make the surgical joining of small blood vessels easier, or nerve repairs, or help with operating on the head or neck. I had said I would do my best to find some and was thinking how I might do that. There was a medical equipment store just around the corner from where I lived in London, so I would walk to them and ask shortly.

I was also restricted to how much luggage I could take with me and had been told I could bring a maximum of two large bags. I had a couple of North Face duffels that fitted the bill nicely, but in addition to any requested medical equipment, I needed to be self-contained and carry with me the food I intended to eat. It sounded as if Gaza would work wonders for my waistline, whatever the risks to my welfare. Rice and canned tuna for a fortnight might end up as a tedious menu, but in a territory when famine was imminent, I could not rely on the locals for anything. I had decided to take everything I needed, just in case. In war one never knew.

Money worried me, not the spending but the possibility of being robbed. I had heard reports of aid workers losing items at checkpoints, or from where they were sleeping. The only valid currencies in Gaza were the Israeli shekel and the US dollar. The UK pound was worthless. I had thus folded loose notes inside a secret money belt around my waist. The belt looked as normal, was made from plastic and would not trigger metal detectors, so I could wear it all the time. I had another wallet that I wore next to my groin, again there was no metal, and yet another hung from my neck but tucked under my shirt. I also had a throw wallet. This was a wallet filled with out-of-date credit and identity cards, and a small quantity of real money. Should I be robbed, mugged, or attacked, I could offer the throw wallet in the hope the assailants would be satisfied, while the real money remained hidden in multiple locations. The wallet around my neck was hard to hide and gave the appearance of a massive paunch. For Gaza, I had to look fat.

Although my luggage had been limited to my two North Face duffels, what I had packed was so overweight it was ludicrous. No sensible airline would have allowed me to check in. One bag weighed 40kg and the other was 35kg. I thought I had everything perfectly arranged but established that I would have to jettison many items that I had earlier regarded as essential.

There was no chance in Gaza that I would be able to wash my clothes. At least I could try to wash them, assuming sufficient water, but drying them would be a challenge as I would be spending much of my time under cover. It was not the environment to go for an outdoor walk or hang up my clearly foreign clothes on a line for drying. That would attract too much attention, so I had to take enough clothes to wash nothing at all until I returned. That would be a challenge, especially as my clearly excess baggage weight obliged me to discard at least a quarter of what I had packed. I was likely to be rather smelly when I had finished my time in Gaza.

Meanwhile my mobile telephone had been ringing almost continuously.

"I know you are busy but…," said one caller.

"I won't take a moment," said another.

"Just before you go," said a third.

Friends were also ringing to wish me well, even if I had not told them I was going to Gaza, and plenty had said I was in their prayers. I had not even left the UK, but already had seven different religions praying for me – Christianity, Islam, Hinduism, Buddhism, Judaism, Taoism, and even a Scientologist. I found that odd, as God-fearing was not something at which I excelled, and I had told almost no one where I was going. Yet the word was out. I had no clue how.

Key to my success in Gaza was for me to remain healthy. I could not afford to become ill. Under normal circumstances, the incidence of traveller's diarrhoea in Egypt, through which I would be passing, is at least 60 per cent. This figure would be even higher for Gaza. All five of Gaza's wastewater treatment plants and most of its 65 sewage pumping stations had been forced to close, so gastroenteritis was likely to be common and cholera not far away. Had I been inoculated? I fear not. I had to rely on good sense and fortune to keep me healthy.

Filled with thoughts of Gaza, and yet still wishing to relax, I met with an ex-Army colleague for lunch and although it was a pleasure to meet, I worried about our timing. While I had decided to stop listening to news bulletins and pretend I was going somewhere peaceful, and despite seven religions praying for my welfare, my colleague had experiences of warfare that made Indiana Jones look tame. Our conversation rapidly changed to conflict and the dangers of being at a frontline. He had been blown up by an Improvised Explosive Device (IED) in Afghanistan several years earlier and had suffered the mental effects of that ever since. I was unsure that his was a story I should be hearing, only days before I was scheduled to enter Gaza. We both sipped alcohol-free beer and I listened to his tales, while we tucked in to lunch. By the time we reached dessert, the conclusion was clear. I was crazy to even contemplate entering Gaza, yet there was no way I would be backing down.

We bade each other farewell and with my stomach full I made my slow way on foot across London. I still had to find the operating loupes. Surprisingly, this task was simple, as the supplier near to where I lived had plenty. Once he heard where the loupes were headed, he instantly reduced his price by 15 per cent, which made me buy two pairs. He was happy, I was happy, and I was sure Gaza would be happy, too. All I had to do was get the loupes there without being arrested for carrying suspicious items. In both Egypt and Gaza, with a war in full swing, suspicious items made you a spy, unless you could prove differently. In conflict you were guilty until proved innocent, which was precisely how it should not be.

Packing the new loupes into North Face duffels that were already overladen was a challenge. Eventually, I removed several pairs of socks, at least half my underwear, and two shirts, so the operating loupes would have a new home. Had I removed anything further, I would have been entering Gaza naked, not the best way of blending into the background. However, the operating loupes ended up tightly packed among my possessions headed to Gaza, and I could only hope I would be able to take them the whole way.

Since the war began, several items destined for Gaza had gone missing and Egyptian Customs were at times being understanding while at others they were heavy handed. Some aid organisations were having their equipment impounded at Cairo Airport if documentation could not be produced to certify that the equipment they had imported was for humanitarian purposes and not being sold on the Black Market. Medical Aid for Palestinians was not the only organisation trying to assist Gaza. There were many others doing what they could, and most were simply getting on with things and trying not to be noticed. Even at times of conflict, documentation must be watertight. I had yet to find a war zone that was different.

Preparing for Gaza required me to do plenty of walking, it seemed almost from one side of London to the other. I glanced at the pedometer that I wore routinely. By the time I had dropped onto my sagging bed, and before I fell asleep, I had walked 13.5 kilometres (8.4 miles) between dawn and dusk. No one could say I was being lazy. Londoners, it was said, walked further each day than the residents of any other UK city. I was living evidence of that.

\* \* \*

Chapter 2

# The Team Assembles

Despite me trying not to listen to the news, I occasionally slipped up. That was how I heard of the two unarmed teenage Palestinians waving white flags who had been shot and killed in Gaza. To compound the event, a digger had been filmed scooping up the bodies and burying them in a mound of waste. I had thought the war could not become worse, but I was clearly wrong. The depravity of those responsible horrified me.

Most reports were from foreign journalists near to Gaza, but not inside. Just a few were from within the territory itself and there was barely any UK media representation there at all. Journalists had experienced a high rate of attrition in Gaza with 103 being killed in the first five months of the war. That was appalling. I sensed it was intentional, especially as there was manifestly a widespread move to pressurise the public to hold a specific opinion. I had no idea how the bigwigs thought this would work, as it was bound to backfire in the end. Once again, I thanked Heaven I was a medic and could focus solely on the injured. It made life simpler for me, albeit in a difficult environment. Razing Gaza to the ground, should that have been the intent, was unquestionably the wrong thing to do, other than it satisfied revenge. The Israel-Palestine conflict had existed for so long that all extreme revenge would do was kick the tin can down the road.

In addition, the modern mobile telephone had created many journalists, albeit untrained. It was barely possible for anything to escape someone with a mobile telephone and for an incident not to be filmed. Many of the events I had already viewed had been filmed by passers-by, and had nothing to do with professional journalists at all.

With such little time to go before heading to Gaza, I was surprised not to have met the other members of my team. Consequently, when an online briefing was proposed by the MAP Communications specialists, I grabbed the opportunity to attend immediately. There were two briefers, one in the West Bank's Ramallah, the other in London. MAP was certainly a medical organisation, with a long track record of work in the Middle East, extending back more than 20 years. It was why I had become involved. However, MAP was also an advocacy group, so the briefers were keen to see if any of the team was prepared to be interviewed by assorted news outlets on our return. The aim was to say nothing until we got back. I put my hat in the ring, as did two others, although one team member declined. Being interviewed after the mission made sense, but we would be the fifth team to enter Gaza in as many months, so I felt it likely that our cover was already blown. The various intelligence agencies that were clearly working overtime to wage war were bound to have worked out what we were doing, who was involved, and the likely media involvement when we returned. It would be no surprise to any of them. The one safe area we had was medical, so each team member had to stay there and not be distracted. I had heard all manner of opinions from armchair warriors over the previous weeks. I was now out of the armchair and headed for the medical frontline and had to be very careful what I said.

Three months earlier, when I had been thinking about going to Gaza, but had to delay because of my shoulder, I felt I had plenty of time to do whatever I wished. Yet with the trip just around the corner, everything suddenly seemed a rush. Thanks to the international nature of the team – we came from several different countries – and with Gaza being two hours ahead of UK time, my mobile telephone was pinging non-stop. What was night-time to me could be daytime to others, so I dared not turn it off at night. I just lay in the darkness and listened to the mobile pinging, as repeated messages hit its screen. Going on a mission to a conflict zone was a busy time, even if I had said I was going walking. I could not see any way of making predeparture relaxing.

I was unable to decide, in what would be a completely Islamic location, whether I should shave. Wet shaving needed water, and Gaza was struggling with supply, so I saw no point in that. Meanwhile, my electric shaver needed charging every few days and was bulky, so I saw little point in that either, especially when the electricity supply was erratic. I eventually decided on a small, battery-powered electric razor that I normally kept for emergencies.

My initial thoughts had been to drive and park at London's Heathrow Airport so that my car was easily available on my return three weeks later. However, because there was a chance events would turn sour, and I had no control over that, I decided to leave my car in central London rather than the airport. In central London the vehicle could be retrieved by a relative or family member in the event of disaster. All I could do was hope this precaution was never required.

Departure anywhere was always about packing, then repacking, and repacking again. There was no logic to it, it was simply the way it was. Perhaps it was a form of therapy. The best way to limit what I took was to restrict the size of bag, as I always filled anything to the hilt. For what must have been the tenth time, I repacked my two North Face duffels, removed a few items that appeared superfluous, scrutinised them carefully, decided I needed them after all, and repacked them once again in the duffels. Did I need four jars of instant coffee? I did not, but the Palestinians in Gaza would be different. Instant coffee to them was a delicacy. Or the antibacterial hand gel that I was sure I would need – was 500mls truly necessary? As for toothpaste, one tube or two? I was fiddling unnecessarily. It was time to get started and take with me what I could.

The end point of packing for any zone of conflict or disaster was to always have everything neat and tidy. In addition, there was the grab-bag. This was a small bag that I kept with me permanently, when I was out and about, in the shower, in bed, on the loo, everywhere. The grab-bag was a critical piece of equipment that was stuffed with sufficient essentials to keep me going if I needed to escape in a hurry. The nature of all zones of conflict was that one never knew what would happen, or when. Events could change in a blink. My grab-bag had helped me on two previous occasions. The first was a Hezbollah roadblock in Lebanon's Bekaa Valley, the second was a tower block fire in Dubai. Without my grab-bag on either occasion, I would have been struggling.

Packing and repacking complete, it was time to relax before my imminent departure. I settled into an armchair, felt relaxation take hold, but jumped at a sudden "Ping!". Another text message had just arrived. I glanced at my overworked mobile's screen. It was a message from a colleague with plentiful experience of war zones. His advice was not the kind to ignore:

> *"Take good care of yourself out there Richard. Don't be afraid to turn around and make the bigger decision of retreating if things are getting too dicey. Watching [the] news there is fierce fighting around the hospitals today. I'm worried that [if] you don't have the military or*

*UN back up you might get caught out. Let me know how things are going if you can. I will be hoping and praying you are okay."*

Wise advice, yet difficult to implement. It was time to get started. There was no going back as there were so many Palestinian injured that needed me.

\* \* \*

I awoke early, after a bad night's sleep. If I had gathered more than four hours of kip that would have been an exaggeration. Before I had gone to bed, I had taken screenshots of all essential documents in the event I was challenged, had also copied them onto a data stick, and had left hard copies in an obvious location in my London flat, in case I did not make it home. I had told no one I had done that, for fear of creating alarm.

I was still trying hard not to listen to the news but for some reason had a morbid fascination to hear what was happening. It was evident that the war was not going away in a hurry and there was plenty of unpleasantness taking place. Gaza's Health Ministry had said that 71 Palestinians had been killed and 112 wounded in the previous 24 hours alone. Mosques had also ceased being protected, as the Saad bin Abi Waqqas Mosque in the Jabalia refugee camp of northern Gaza had been bombed. Hospitals were also being targeted, so there seemed little advantage to being either religious or medical. The rules of war, if such things applied to the Israeli/Palestinian conflict, had clearly changed.

Israel continued to state that it intended to attack Rafah, right by the crossing into Gaza I would be using. However, there were growing calls by US officials that these plans should be cancelled. The Israeli Defence Minister, Yoav Gallant, had recently visited Washington and had been inundated with complaints about the civilian toll in Gaza. He had also received many requests to call off a Rafah invasion. I had no clue how Israel intended to avoid civilian casualties in Rafah if it was to invade as so many displaced people had ended up there, thanks to the fighting further north. Rafah was as far south as they could go.

Predictably perhaps, and barely an hour before I was scheduled to leave for the airport, another request arrived from Gaza. This time it was for adult dialysis lines, and could I find some? Dialysis is the medical process of filtering the blood of waste products if the kidneys cannot do the job when a patient has gone into kidney (renal) failure. A dialysis line is a soft plastic tube, twice the length and half the width of a pen, that is placed through the skin into one of the large veins of the neck or the groin. Once inserted, the line is then connected to the tubes on a haemodialysis machine. This allows blood to be pumped from the body to the machine and back for dialysis. Sadly, the medical supplier who supplied the loupes was not open sufficiently early, so I failed to find dialysis lines for Gaza before I departed for the airport.

The driver who took me to Heathrow talked non-stop, and barely drew breath. On several occasions I had to interrupt him apologetically so that I could make farewell telephone calls but even then, he carried on talking. In one respect I was sorry to see him go, once we arrived at Heathrow, while in others I was relieved. However, I had soon found my way to the departure gate for my flight to Cairo and it was there, for the first time that I physically met other members of the Emergency Medical Team, EMT5. Until that point, I had only met them online.

There was David, the South African anaesthetist, albeit working in the UK's Oxford. He had been working hard throughout the day before, had only finished at 7 p.m. that evening, and had little time to pack.

"It was just as well," he commented. "It gave me less time to worry."

There was Mahim, a vascular surgeon from London. Vascular surgery is an important specialty for a war zone, as shrapnel can so easily damage a blood vessel and destroy the blood supply to a limb, with limb loss being the result. Vascular surgeons act quickly to repair the damaged vessel and are continuously working against the clock. Dozy people do not become vascular surgeons.

Unfortunately, vascular operations can take a long time to perform, which means the surgical wound lies open for this period, and so the risks of infection are increased.

And there was Khaled, a Palestinian general surgeon from London, who had been to Gaza before, only two months earlier.

After our initial introduction, one of the team asked, "Can you take some cigarettes into Gaza?"

Despite me being a profound non-smoker, and disapproving greatly of the habit, I instantly nodded. This was not the moment to make a fruitless point. If we needed to take cigarettes into Gaza, I was delighted to assist. I could see the reason, as a single cigarette in Gaza presently cost US$4. The territory was not the place to be a chain smoker.

Meeting us in Cairo would be two others. Roberto, a vascular surgeon from Rome and Mohammad, a theatre nurse from Amman. Both were highly experienced.

After a trouble-free flight and nearly losing our luggage, we met as a fully assembled team on the roof of our Cairo hotel later that evening. It was the last half of Ramadan, the fasting month of Islam. I was not fasting but some of my colleagues were. I watched them tuck into their evening meal, the *iftar* meal, that evening with real gusto.

We were on our way to Gaza.

\* \* \*

# Chapter 3

# My Name is Abu Ruairidh

After my first day's training in Cairo about the perils facing me in Gaza, I was looking to buy a ticket home. Sadly, I could find nowhere, so it looked as if I would be going to Palestine, regardless of the dangers ahead. I understood that at least one person before me had flown back to the UK from that point and had gone nowhere near Gaza. I could fully understand that decision.

Yet the humanitarian security training, with more to follow, forced me to focus. There was a war taking place in Gaza. It was no comic strip, no casual discussion, it was the real thing. People were dying and being injured in droves. The Israelis had already dropped a missile on one of the team's locations, had done the same for Médecins Sans Frontières (MSF), while three United Nations observers and a translator had recently been wounded in an explosion while on patrol in southern Lebanon. It was clear that neutral parties were being targeted, whatever the rights and wrongs, so anyone inside Gaza could be attacked, whether by accident or design.

Many fine words were being spoken by bigwigs around the world, but I am unsure if any improved life on the ground. The United Nations Interim Force in Lebanon (UNIFIL) had declared that all actors in a conflict had a responsibility under international law to ensure the protection of non-combatants. These included peacekeepers, journalists, medical personnel, and civilians. There appeared to be no chance of such protection in Gaza. In the previous 24 hours, 82 people had been killed and 98 wounded. In Gaza that was a good day. The United States was no help as it had just approved another US$2.5bn to be spent on warplanes and weapons for Israel, despite concerns that Israeli forces would expand their operations to Rafah. The new arms package included more than 1800 MK84 2,000-pound bombs and 500 MK82 500-pound bombs. A 2,000-pound bomb could cause injury up to 300 metres away and had been linked to earlier mass casualty events in Gaza. Israel was also expanding its operations against Hezbollah, hence its attacks in southern Lebanon, and had declared it would reach Hezbollah from wherever it operated.

Apart from my security training, the day was also the 48th anniversary of Land Day and about 10,000 Palestinians had marched across Israel to mark the moment. Land Day memorialises 30 March 1976 when Israeli forces shot and killed six Palestinians who protested the Israeli regime's confiscation of tens of thousands of dunams of Palestinian land. A dunam is 1,000 square metres of land and is a unit of measurement used since the era of the British Mandate of Palestine. There are 4.05 acres to one dunam. Each year, Palestinians across the world memorialise Land Day.

Part of the training was to also be reminded of the basic principles of humanitarian work. These were important, for they might be the only things that prevented a humanitarian worker from being harmed. The principles were neutrality, impartiality, humanity, and independence. The four words should be engraved on every humanitarian's heart. Gaza was apparently now showing an element of Palestinian-on-Palestinian injury, as its social structure fell apart. Criminal violence was also rising fast.

To make humanitarian work as safe as possible, and there were no assurances given by Israel, there was a process known as *deconfliction*. This required the movements of staff and vehicles to be cleared first by the Israelis. If deconfliction of an area was not permitted, it could mean that Israel would be operational in that location, either then or imminently. Deconfliction did not mean an attack would never happen. It simply meant that a combatant would try and prevent accidental attack. Deconfliction also did not apply to Hamas.

We were taught that surveillance by many different actors was always taking place in Gaza and was particularly looking out for odd patterns of behaviour. For example, most of us had already disconnected ourselves from any form of social media activity before leaving the UK, but one of us had not done so. They were immediately told to do nothing about it, as the action could raise suspicion. I was told that I should expect to be regarded as a spy throughout my time in Gaza, even though I was not, and be extremely careful about anything I photographed. My ticket back home to the UK at that moment did seem very attractive.

As the training proceeded, I could see the team become increasingly silent. It was not boredom but focus, especially when we were taught what to do when a grenade was lobbed in our direction. I noticed the tutors said "when" not "if". Basically, I was to lie face down, keep my passport visible above my head, and cross my legs at the ankles, to reduce the area of body exposed. When a grenade explodes, the fragments go upwards and outwards, so there was a chance that when one detonated, it could miss me. Admittedly the chances were small, but they still existed.

How could any humanitarian medic cope with such information? The problem was that I was required do so, as shortly I would be in Gaza for real. There were clear perils ahead and although our training staff reassured us that we could opt out at any time, it was evident there was no going back.

Weapons were also an issue, as in some Middle Eastern lands it was normal to see locals touting weapons almost anywhere. Today's Gaza was different. The only individuals with weapons were the fighters, so I was instructed to avoid anyone with a weapon. The same applied to uniforms, as any uniformed official could be a target. Gaza was not the place to seek a policeman's help if I ran into trouble. I was unlikely to ever see one, but if I did, the message was to steer clear.

There was one simple rule of thumb for Gaza.. The person in charge was the one with the weapon. I was to never question them, but just do what they might say. And bribes? I had used them in many lands, but Gaza had carried little cash since the war began, so I was to forget bribes as a way of greasing palms. I was to get in, get out, and attract as little attention as I could.

After repeated packings of my North Face duffel bags in London, I felt I had all I would need for Gaza. The Cairo team disagreed, and delivered another huge, unexpected load of items. There were five pairs of operating theatre scrub clothes, surgeons call them *scrubs*, five surgical hats, 80 wet wipes, a packet of cotton wool, toothpaste, soap, shampoo, a loofah, loo paper, nail clippers, and a pack of 100 cotton earbuds. I had no idea what to do with any of them, especially the loofah.

In preparation for my crossing into Gaza, I was also given an Arab name. I was no longer me, but I became Al Hajj Ghalib Abu Ruairidh, or Abu Ruairidh for short. Al Hajj suggested age and wisdom. I was unsure about the wisdom although I was sure about the age. Ghalib meant that I was victorious, while Abu Ruairidh was thanks to my eldest son. I was the only person on the team with a real UK background and

I did not look remotely like an Arab. For Gaza, I was unsure whether that was good or bad, but I was taking no chances.

Our training also considered mental health, on the basis that in Gaza we were assured to see horrors. Online with a tutor from the US I was asked to consider what acute manifestations of stress I might be showing. I had plenty – disturbed sleep, occasional memory loss, suspiciousness, difficulty with concentration, and an altered sense of reality. When I have returned to the UK from conflict zones on earlier occasions, I have considered myself to be normal, but those near to me have thought otherwise. To them, I have changed, and it can take me several weeks to return to what they regard as normal.

I was also given a 54321 grounding exercise, which involved saying to myself:

> Give 5 things I can see, 4 things I can feel, 3 things I can hear, 2 things I can smell, and 1 thing I can taste.

So, I did, at least I tried. Seeing five things was not a problem but feeling four was difficult, especially because I was wearing wet socks. I was having difficulty drying them in my hotel's air-conditioned room, so all I could feel and smell were soggy socks. I gave up the 54321 grounding exercise shortly afterwards. Wet socks had ruined my attempt.

Apparently in case I relaxed, as our training was a succession of horror topics, each of which we had to understand, we also underwent Stop the Bleed training. This was critical as approximately 25 per cent of those who die in conflict need not have done so and perish simply from bleeding out. They could have been saved if bleeding had been controlled. It was a sobering thought that if I walked around a Commonwealth War Graves cemetery, a quarter of the headstones need not have been there. The control of haemorrhage was an essential skill. As a surgeon I had seen plenty of bleeding, for that is what happens during an operation. However, Stop the Bleed training was about how to control haemorrhage when out and about, maybe at a checkpoint, or simply when travelling from one location to another.

Consequently, we practised putting tourniquets on both each other and ourselves, as well as plugging the hole created by a sucking chest wound. Once done, I placed a fluorescent orange tourniquet and a tiny packet of compressed gauze in a zipped pocket of my gilet. The tourniquet and gauze were for my use, not for anyone else, so each team member carried their tourniquet and gauze in the same pocket as me. Should a colleague be shot and bleeding, I was not about to lend them my tourniquet, nor was I expecting them to lend me theirs. Tourniquets were like a grab bag. They were kept close by, and instantly accessible, as the response to control haemorrhage must be instant. It would take all of three minutes to bleed out from a major artery. Reaction must be immediate.

Our pre-Gaza training complete, the team felt ready to do what was needed and we were instructed to be packed and on board our transport by 3:30 a.m. in the morning. To reach Gaza's Rafah crossing meant first crossing Egypt's Sinai Peninsula, which could only be done in convoy as the area was demilitarised. There were 46 vehicles scheduled to form the convoy. Anyone who reported late for the start of the convoy would be left behind. Once at the Rafah crossing, the convoy leader would turn round and return to Cairo. Thereafter we would be on our own.

Then the bombshell hit. A sombre-faced Tibetan begged our silence for a few minutes and then broke the news. We had no insurance, he declared, so would be unable to enter Gaza for at least another 24 hours, possibly longer. I could barely believe what I was being told. Nor did I feel he was telling us the truth, he certainly looked unconvinced himself, but I had to go with what was being said. I felt strongly his was a fabricated excuse, an attempt to slow down, or even prevent, our entry into Gaza.

Despite our alleged lack of insurance, and almost on the spur of that moment, we decided to leave Cairo as planned, but to stop in a town called Arish, one hour before the Rafah crossing. It would allow us to dash to Gaza once it was permitted as the territory would not be far away.

As if to confirm my thoughts about fabrication, a short while later I heard that Israel had bombed the courtyard of the hospital to which I was headed, the Al Aqsa Hospital in the city of Deir-al-Balah. Seven journalists, including one working for the BBC, were injured and four members of the Islamic Jihad (IJ) militant group had been killed. The Israelis claimed they had struck an IJ command centre in the grounds of the hospital. This was the first I had heard of the hospital being used as an IJ command centre and this certainly had not featured in our pre-Gaza briefings. We were generally advised that it would be unlikely for us ever to see a fighter. If we were ever asked to see one, it was likely that the area would first be cleared of all lookers-on and we would see the individual in private. Islamic Jihad apart, the injured journalists were among hundreds of Palestinians sheltering in makeshift tents in the grounds of the hospital and they were not operating as journalists at all.

The more I learned about the bombing of the hospital, the less I believed the excuse that it was a lack of insurance that was restricting our entry into Gaza. What was more, the Emergency Medical Team before us had just left, while our team had yet to arrive. What a perfect time to bomb a hospital without risk to foreigners from countries that claimed to support Israel. I will never know, but my antennae of suspicion were raised. In war, anything was feasible, and nothing was ever what it seemed.

\* \* \*

Chapter 4

# The Human Shield in Arish

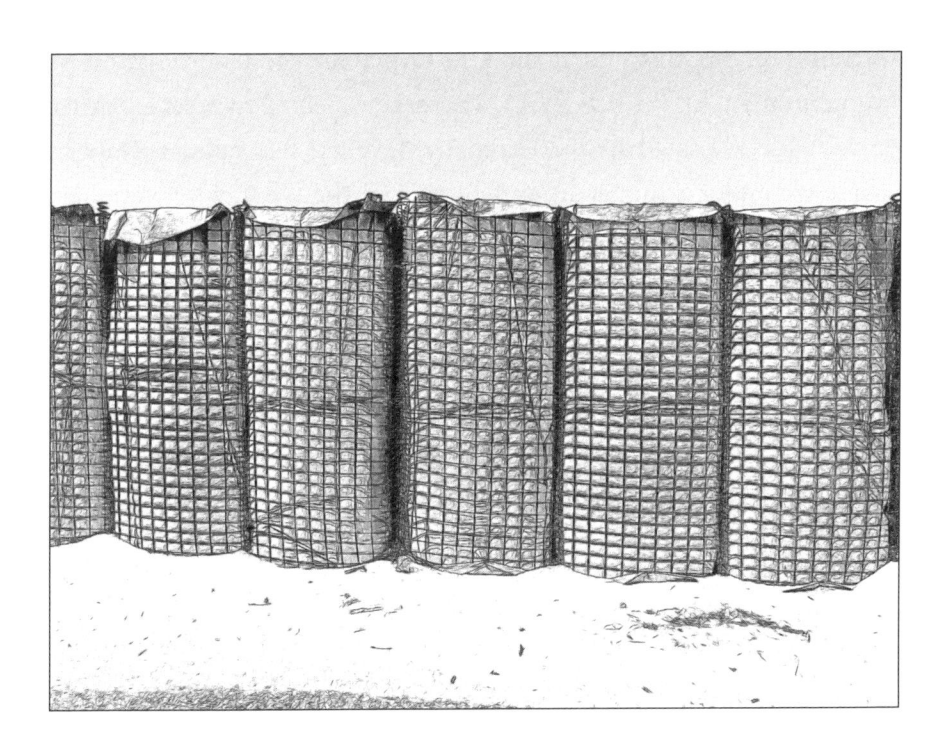

I was not sure that April Fool's Day was an appropriate date to be heading towards Gaza, but that was what it was. I was woken by the faintest knock on my door in what felt to be the middle of the night. It was. I glanced at my watch, it was 2:30 a.m., and without thinking I leaped from the bed, took the few steps to the door, and flung it open. It was only then I realised I was not wearing a stitch.

"Minibar?" said the night porter, who was standing just outside the door. "Please can I see it?"

He never once looked down and was out of my room in a jiffy, having recorded that I had taken nothing, so worried had I been by the pre-Gaza training. It was a bare 30-minute drive through early-morning Cairo, our team of six distributed between three minibuses, plus a huge quantity of baggage. Somehow one of my colleagues had acquired 18 suitcases filled with goodies for the deprived Palestinian population that we would shortly be joining. No one complained. Our first rendezvous was at the UN Office for the Coordination of Humanitarian Affairs (OCHA), where we expected to meet a further 43 vehicles. We saw barely 20 as many travellers had failed to appear. There were two orthopaedic surgeons from the USA, who were part of a larger group that had been told they would be too many to cross into Gaza that day, so would have to wait another 48 hours before entering. My antennae of suspicion raised still further when I heard this. We had been delayed because of an apparent lack of insurance, the American surgeons had been delayed because their group was too large, and nearly half of the vehicles for the convoy had not appeared for reasons that were unclear. Something was going on, but I was unsure what.

One man did appear for the briefing and was allowed through. He was carrying nearly three dozen eggs and was headed for an organisation in Gaza called World Central Kitchen. Sadly, he would be dead within 24 hours.

The war continued. Israel had withdrawn its forces from Gaza City's Al Shifa Hospital, in the north of the land, having undertaken a military operation there for two weeks. The Israel Defence Force (IDF) had claimed it had killed and captured numerous Hamas fighters and that the raid was one of the most successful operations of its Gaza war. It claimed that 900 people suspected of being militants had been arrested, as well as weapons, valuable intelligence, and more than US$3 million in different currencies seized. Local witnesses had said that the hospital was in ruins and that hundreds of bodies of killed civilians had been found. People there were trying to salvage what they could, as Al Shifa Hospital had also been a shelter for IDPs.

# The Human Shield in Arish    29

Reports from southern Gaza, where I was headed, were that the situation was dire. The main attacks had been in the city of Khan Yunis, but the prediction was that there would shortly be expansion of the fighting further south in the territory, and that meant Rafah.

There were many checkpoints on our way eastwards across the Sinai Peninsula to Arish, some speedy, some slow. The Sinai Peninsula was a demilitarised area and started almost immediately after the road from Cairo passed beneath the Suez Canal. Each checkpoint had several armed guards, and one even had a machine gun at the ready, ammunition belt in place, although the weapon was pointing towards the Mediterranean Sea for reasons I could not understand. Meanwhile at another checkpoint I saw a rifle range, albeit infrequently used, while there was body armour visible at all the points we stopped. Sometimes it was being worn while at others was hanging nearby, but the checkpoints were clearly at the ready.

The Sinai Peninsula was not all barren desert and was manifestly an active region. There were trees at many of the checkpoints, eucalyptus especially, as well as active birdlife. I saw a swallow at one point, too, diving low and swooping past me, unsurprising when the temperature as we drove was around 34°C. There were spots of agricultural land visible here and there, and frequent salt flats. The locals of the Sinai Peninsula were mostly Bedouin and there were many military encampments on the way, although most had unmanned guard towers. There were empty apartment blocks, too, waiting for the day when they may have to be filled with soldiers, in the event of another attack. In 1967, Israel conquered the Sinai Peninsula, but handed it back 15 years later after the Camp David Accords of 1978, the small southerly territory of Taba excepted.

Disappointingly, mankind was having its effect, which was not a pretty sight. There was a huge quantity of plastic debris, littered either side of the road and extending far into the desert. It looked as if it had never been cleared. There was plenty of aid intended for Gaza but very little moving. For much of the route across the Sinai Peninsula there were large aid lorries parked each side of the road, and narrowing the roadway. This surprised me, as some of the items waiting to be delivered were bound to be perishable and would deteriorate in the heat.

Before this war, Gaza was receiving 500 truckloads of deliveries each day. Now, during the war, Gaza had seen an average of 112 lorries daily. A truckload of aid was far more efficient than any alternative form of provision. Parachute resupply might have seemed spectacular but was limited and dangerous. Already plenty of Palestinians had been crushed by parachutes that failed to open. Helicopters had also been used but could only carry a minuscule payload. Aircraft were useful but could not equal the carrying capacities of trucks and Gaza had no functioning airstrip anyway, while items had still to be delivered by some means to their point of distribution.

Ships were also possible, and the USA was constructing a harbour. Yet even a ship could not compete with lorries. Ultimately, the solution was to increase the number of lorries to Gaza as much as possible, and soon if famine was to be avoided.

By 10:30 a.m. we had pulled into a hotel in Arish and were rapidly given rooms. Arish, which lay on Egypt's coast, was like so many of the world's war zones. It was the last piece of reasonable normality before entering a zone of conflict. Many of the people I had seen in the Arishes of the world would say they were there for one reason, but their true role was different. Arish was where trust stopped, and reality began, as Gaza was not far away. I was pleased to find that there was some surgical support at Arish port. It was there that the UAE had berthed a 200-bedded floating hospital, which was receiving and treating injured Palestinians from Gaza. Two hundred beds might sound a lot but for the Gaza conflict it was the tipmost tip of a massive iceberg.

That evening, I smoked a *shisha* pipe with an American, who also happened to be staying in the hotel. He came directly up to me and introduced himself, which immediately made me suspicious. *Shisha* is a good way of encouraging discussions about all manner of topics. The American said that he was a member of the US Diplomatic Security

Service (DSS) and was clearly well travelled. He had worked in lands whose names I could barely pronounce. He formed part of a seven-person team and was on a 36-month posting. Good luck to him in Arish, I thought. It was bad enough being there for 36 hours, but 36 months? That needed serious self-discipline. The DSS was the main security and law enforcement agency of the United States Department of State, its primary mission being to provide security for diplomatic assets, personnel, and information. It also had a strong cyber protective function. The American, who was charming, asked plenty of questions and was keen to understand why we were in Arish at all. We told him most things, but not everything. I wager what we said made it back to the USA in double-quick time, likely even before bedtime. But that was why places like Arish existed. They were where stranger could meet stranger while information and even money could be exchanged in reasonable safety. Places like Arish were critical to the running of any war.

\* \* \*

When I awoke the next morning, I felt terrible, likely the after-effects of the *shisha*. I forgot to shave, and bounced off several walls in my room as I made my way to the bathroom, so decided to clear my head by walking along the beach immediately beside the hotel. The walk helped clear my mind and bring life to my aching brain but the moment I returned to the hotel 45 minutes later, I received the news from last night. There were problems.

The IDF had killed an international team of seven aid workers from World Central Kitchen (WCK) with several missiles launched late last night. Those killed were from Palestine, Australia, Poland, the UK, and a US-Canada citizen. One of them was the man with the eggs I had seen in Cairo. The attack had been near to Deir-al-Balah in Central Gaza, which was precisely where I was headed. The WCK vehicle had followed the rules and was officially deconflicted, which meant the IDF would have known ahead of time where the vehicle would be. Granted, it was late, but deconfliction should have taken care of that. When I looked at the images of one of the vehicles after the attack, there was a single hole through the roof of the car and complete destruction within, but the overall shape of the vehicle remained. It struck me as a missile launched for assassination, nothing more and nothing less. Whatever different spokesmen might have said, the killing would have been intentional. To me, it was also a further reason why our entry into Gaza had been delayed, on the back of a so-called lack of insurance. The Israelis wanted foreigners out of the way so they could create their deadly mischief before allowing us in. Insurance lack? No chance. It was always just an excuse.

The outcry globally about the WCK killings was huge, and I felt there was a chance that our mission into Gaza would be further postponed or even cancelled. We met as a team to consider what had happened. The mood was not good.

My view was straightforward. Everything we had so far witnessed had been for a reason. Perhaps it was because I was an ex-soldier, but it seemed sensible that we had primary and secondary missions. Our primary mission was clear. We were headed for Al Aqsa Hospital to shore up emergency support. However, war could be incredibly foggy, so we needed a secondary mission in reserve, in case our primary mission fell apart, for whatever cause. It would manifestly be a risk to go to the hospital in Deir-al-Balah so if we could not reach it, a secondary mission could be for us to set up a programme of next steps for healthcare in Gaza. It was apparent that hospitals were being primarily targeted, so longer term care might have to be outside the territory. Our secondary mission could be to develop that. Outside Gaza, it would be easier to provide long-term care and rehabilitation. It would mean specialist surgery, rehabilitation, prosthetics, microbiology, imaging, haematology, biochemistry, blood transfusion, and plenty more. Such things could not be achieved in anything other than a proper hospital, but planning had to begin there and then. Sadly, I sensed my views fell on deaf ears. The full focus was on our primary mission.

As if to reinforce the perilous dangers facing Gaza's hospitals, MSF had said that Gaza City's Al Shifa Hospital was in ruins, one day after Israeli troops withdrew from the complex. The IDF had also recently attacked a consular building in Damascus that belonged to the Islamic Republic of Iran, killing several individuals, including at least two Islamic Revolutionary Guard Corps (IRGC) commanders. Such buildings were seen as the property of a country, so Israel's attacks were interpreted as being the same as an attack on Iran itself. One could expect retaliation to occur. It was clear the war was hotting up, not cooling down. We were also about to go forward towards the conflict, not back. Meanwhile, global public opinion was becoming very critical of Israel's unapologetic killings, in many different locations, and politicians supporting the stance were becoming slowly alienated.

The airwaves and internet were filled with an increasing clamour for Israel to justify and explain the WCK killings, as the assassination of seven aid workers was inexcusable. Israel's Prime Minister, Benjamin Netanyahu had admitted his forces launched the air raid and called it unintended and tragic. I could not see how his words could have reassured the families of those who had perished.

Meanwhile peace talks persisted, and I continued to hope that something positive would come from them. A new truce proposal had been drafted by Israeli negotiators in Egypt, which would be sent to Hamas for their views. I was unable to influence anything at all but found myself grasping at straws and hoping that all would settle. From the outside I was perhaps seen as bold. On the inside I was flapping. As if to demonstrate that the war would run and run, Iran's Supreme Leader Khamenei had also said that Israel would be punished for their attack on the Iranian consulate in Syria's Damascus. In more peaceful support, Spain had also declared it would recognise Palestinian statehood by July. With all these words, I continued to wonder if any of the various bigwigs had ever visited Gaza at all. Perhaps they would have spoken differently had they done so.

Events were clearly moving apace. At our local, much simpler level, we still had to work out if it would be safe to enter Gaza at all. We checked with those already in the territory, the ground staff who really were exposed to constant danger. They were remarkable people. They said that it should still be safe to enter, which was what we wished to hear. Within moments of receiving their message, I received the instruction to be ready to move. We would be off at 8:00 a.m.

The hotel had filled up with people while we had been establishing our next steps. They were largely evacuees from Gaza who were headed to Qatar by flying from Arish Airport. They were mainly women and children with the very occasional young adult male. Many were amputees and plenty had chronic infections. Post-operative surgical infection was a huge problem in Gaza, unsurprisingly perhaps. Although in the UK I would have regarded an infection rate of 0.25 per cent as too high – orthopaedic surgeons worldwide are known to be neurotic about infection – while a UK general surgeon might see 10 per cent as acceptable, the 100 per cent infection rate being reported from Gaza was horrific. Everything became infected, such were the conditions under which injuries were being treated.

By chance at Arish, as I was busily repacking my already packed duffels, and I still had not decided if I needed one tube of toothpaste or two, I got talking to a cardiologist from Gaza City's Al Shifa Hospital. He was part of the group headed for Qatar although I saw his departure from Gaza was a deep and inner personal wrench for him.

"I will go back," he said on several occasions. He had been married for six months to his lawyer wife and it had cost him US$10,000 to get through the same border as I would shortly be crossing for free, albeit in the opposite direction.

All I could do was nod and wonder how much of Gaza would be remaining if the bombing continued as it was. By the time he decided to return, perhaps in two years' time, there would be a real risk nothing would be left. There was deep guilt emanating from him, as he constantly referred to the family and friends he had left behind in Gaza.

His words shook me. While at Al Shifa Hospital he had been used as a human shield, had seen corpses shifted by digger, and had been aggressively questioned by Israeli forces, who asked him where he had been on 7 October 2023 and whether he had seen any tunnels. He replied that he had been at home that day and had never seen a tunnel. He was unsure if they believed him. He had been told to go ahead of a group of Israeli soldiers who had been tasked to clear the hospital of any supposed Hamas fighters. The doctor was ordered to open each door ahead of the soldiers and would be shot by them had he not complied. The soldiers found nothing.

"How many doctors have been killed at Al Shifa Hospital?" I asked.

"I am aware of 84 doctors killed and 140 academics," he replied. "That number will be increasing further right now."

It was difficult for me to know how to reply, so astonished was I by the numbers. The cardiologist felt there was an attempt by Israel to dumb down the Palestinian population. It was clear the doctor had been deeply traumatised by what he had experienced, and it would take him a very long time to recover, even if he could recover at all. He appeared to welcome talking about his experiences, was going to contact Al Jazeera, the news outlet, and was also going to write a book. Even so, I could tell that he would need copious therapy over many months, probably years. His stories were not fictional, they were completely real and humbling.

I shook his hand in the end before he went back to his room and wife. "Let me shake the hand of a strong man," I said.

The cardiologist's handshake was firm, not what I was expecting, and he looked me confidently in the eyes. I could see the handshake pleased him, as had the opportunity to talk. He then gave the tiniest of smiles and went on his way.

\* \* \*

# Chapter 5

# Into Gaza

However much travelling I did, however efficient I considered myself to be, I was always in a rush before leaving. My Arish departure was no exception. My careful plans seemed suddenly incomplete, so I grabbed a rushed hotel breakfast and then started packing the vans that would take us to Rafah.

The hotel offered someone to help, whom I sensed was a secret policeman, largely because of his leather bomber jacket. I have never seen a hotel porter in a leather bomber jacket before. He was charming but moving suitcases did not appear to be his thing.

Arish had several individuals who claimed to be secret policemen, openly declaring the fact to me, but then whispering, "It is actually secret."

Secrecy in Arish was clearly different to that I had encountered previously.. But it was Arish, and on the margins of a war zone, so everything was unpredictable, understandably so.

We had gathered a huge number of suitcases, largely thanks to one of my colleagues, who was also dressed in black, in addition to a Palestinian *keffiyeh*. This was the wrap-around head covering widely worn by Palestinian men. My colleague, who looked to be the archetypal Hamas supporter thanks to what he was wearing, assured me that the baggage would stay behind in Gaza once we had finished our mission. The suitcases weighed a ton, many of their rolling wheels had broken, as had most of the handles. Meanwhile, I had my two North Face duffels, one black and one red, that I called my wife and daughter bags, respectively. The locals enjoyed and understood that.

Before we left Arish, I was contacted by two ex-military colleagues in the UK, both with PTSD from their time serving in Afghanistan. They declared that they had decided not to listen to the news because they knew I was in Gaza. My presence in or near a war zone was acting as a trigger for their symptoms. I would never have guessed this, although it did seem logical, so I reminded myself to be careful what I told folk back home. I recalled my father, who was in the Navy in the Second World War, telling me a long time ago that those at home had a much worse time than those at the frontline. He was right. I should have thought and had failed to do so.

It was a short drive to the Rafah crossing from Arish, through the remaining desert wastelands of the Sinai Peninsula. On occasion there were classic sand dunes but mostly the landscape was sand and rock almost as far as I could see. Plastic debris continued to be a problem and lay all around, sometimes more than 300 metres from the roadside, evidence of mankind's thoughtless damage to our one-and-only planet. It was a Bedouin area, with ramshackle dwellings dotted here and there on the desertscape, the occasional camel, but little else.

As he drove, my driver played Quranic *surah* loudly in quadrophonic stereo while Mohammad, a near-qualified *hafiz*, kept pace with the words. A *hafiz* was someone who had completely memorised the Quran, which was no simple undertaking. It was more common than one might expect. A *surah* was a chapter – there were 114 in total. From what I could tell, the *surah* were broadcast so as to offer protection for the driver, who could then drive at frenetic speed and make mobile calls simultaneously, while staying close to his Maker. It may have been that the normal side of the road on which to drive in Egypt was the right, but for much of the journey our driver was wandering everywhere, sometimes right, sometimes left, occasionally off road completely. The best thing I could do was close my eyes and pretend to mouth the words of the *surah*.

It was Ramadan, an important religious occasion, and a time for Christians to maintain a low profile in Muslim countries. Ramadan demanded fasting from dawn until sunset and was regarded as one of the Five Pillars of Islam. It lasted 29-30 days, from one sighting of the crescent moon to the next. For a Christian, it was best to join in at Ramadan, and fast as well, rather than insist Christianity was different. I did the best I could, which was not always perfect. My Muslim colleagues were incredibly tolerant when I would sometimes slip up. Full credit to them.

The Sinai Peninsula was rich in military barracks, as well as many abandoned buildings, some pockmarked by shrapnel, others not. There was one location where all the buildings had been destroyed by previous conflict and were lying as ruined rubble. Near to the Gaza border was a line of armoured vehicles, many quite dated, but each glisteningly clean. Their barrels were pointed towards Gaza, as if waiting for an inevitable invasion.

There were many police armoured cars on the route as well, their doors open towards Gaza, also waiting for the expected assault. The Sinai Peninsula had been part of Egypt since roughly 3000 BCE and was the only part of the country located in Asia. It was conquered and occupied by Israel during the Six-Day War of 1967 but mostly handed back after the Camp David Accords 11 years later.

There were multiple checkpoints on the way, with an especially long stop near a town named Sheikh Zuweid. Immediately beside the checkpoint was a high and lengthy concrete defensive wall. I had no idea what happened at these checkpoints but those manning them appeared to understand what they were doing, even if it was a mystery to me. My passport would disappear for long periods, in the hands of a stranger I had barely met, I would worry persistently, and then a smiling official appeared, handed me my passport, I would sigh with relief and move on. I had never been separated so long from my passport as on this journey, but astonishingly everything that was taken from me was eventually returned.

One thing not to do while waiting anywhere, for any reason, in either the Sinai Peninsula or Gaza, was to take photographs, even if there was plenty of opportunity. The moment a camera featured, those around could either steal it or suspect the photographer of being a foreign agent, or both. It was why so many of my photographs during my time in Gaza were fleeting shots. They were all the situation allowed.

How we achieved it, I did not know, but likely thanks to some invisible hand, I fear not thanks to the driver, we made it to the Rafah crossing in what felt to be moments. It was probably about 90 minutes.

The Rafah crossing was a lesson in patience, and I was uncertain I passed the test. My passport disappeared once again, as had become routine, my bags were unpacked, searched, x-rayed, and repacked without anything being challenged, my passport stamped, and my photograph and fingerprints taken. Much of this took place in a large hall, with seating for at least 400. Thanks to the ongoing war, however, barely ten seats were occupied, and six of those were ours.

It took an age for my wife and daughter bags to appear, and at several points I thought I had lost them. However, I was eventually delivered to a time-expired bus that was waiting in No Man's Land and I saw my duffels being packed away in its hold. I had been worrying about my baggage throughout the journey, as items did disappear unexpectedly, and in a blink, at the Rafah crossing. I had received several earlier reports of this happening to other teams, so checked and rechecked everything I was taking into Gaza, and at every opportunity.

"Can anyone hear the drones?" someone asked. I was immediately dragged from my daydreams and looked skywards but saw nothing, other than clear blue sky and a distant whisp of cloud, somewhere to the far north. At least I thought it was a cloud and not a plume of smoke from a recent bombing.

"Not yet," answered another. Everyone shook their heads.

From No Man's Land it was a short drive to the Palestinian side, albeit in the time-expired bus that screeched and bumped its way to Gaza. It was a wonder, I thought, that the bus made it at all. Its market value must have been zero. I could not establish its true colour, although it was likely off-white, as it was covered with plenty of scratches and dents, one merging into the other imperceptibly. Despite the bus doing its best to prevent us, we eventually reached the Palestinian side of the crossing, were cheerfully welcomed by some fit, healthy and well-dressed locals, thanked openly for coming in the middle of a war, were further searched, and moments later were through into Gaza itself.

Once again, I looked up at the clear and light blue sky to see if I could spot a drone. Nothing. There were no drones, no sounds of fighting, while in a far corner was a stack of packaged aid, I suspected flour, waiting for its onward passage to somewhere in deeper Gaza. At the Rafah crossing there was no sign of warfare at all, although I did receive a public disciplining for trying to take a photograph. I wanted a shot of our arrival and simply had not thought.

"Don't!" shouted our Security.

Guiltily, I tried to hide my digital camera, as if I had never intended to take a photograph at all.

"Remember who is in charge here," Security continued. "They'll have you instantly if they think you are taking surveillance images. They are not known for being tolerant or gentle."

Security was right. I was in a Hamas area, and they would have had no clue who I was, or why I was visiting. From their viewpoint I was just a stranger taking photographs, for reasons they might not understand. It was important not to appear suspicious. Onlookers could only judge me by what they saw, not by how I was thinking.

Swiftly I placed my camera in my pocket, whistled and hummed in an attempt to look innocent, and hoped Hamas had not noticed. I suspected that was wishful thinking.

Our transport into central Rafah had not arrived, so we found an area in which to sit, and away from prying eyes. Despite this, two men claiming to be journalists from ABC News appeared as if from nowhere to ask for an interview. Our Security sent them packing, which is probably just as well, as there was no evidence they were genuine journalists and no point in publicising our arrival too loudly. The journalists protested for at least ten minutes, but then gave up and went on their way. I could not tell if their protests were genuine or fabricated. If the latter, they were very good actors.

I made the error of getting into the wrong transport initially, as the UN had arrived with a special armoured minibus, which I had thought had been allocated to me. No chance. I took a seat inside, along with my wife and daughter bags, but was allowed to remain seated in the bulletproof van for barely a minute, before its driver turned to me and said, "This one is not for you." There was a visiting UN bigwig for whom he was waiting and that was definitely not me. Bigwigs got bulletproof vehicles. Lesser mortals such as me did not.

One hour later, two 4x4 unarmoured vehicles arrived. A lack of armour was known as being *soft-skinned*. They were scratched and dented like most vehicles in Gaza and carried a tatty sign on the roof declaring "MAP". This was meant to be visible to overhead drones. I could barely read the sign from the ground, so I worried about a drone, thousands of feet above. Within a short time, we had packed the vehicles with our bags and were headed towards central Rafah.

After barely 50 metres, and before we emerged through the final gate that led into Rafah itself, we were accosted by four young men, each armed with a homemade, wooden club. They were trying to steal any aid that was entering Rafah. Fortunately, they became more interested in a lorry carrying flour that was immediately ahead of us, so we kept our doors locked and windows closed and were through and past in moments. Had it not been for the lorryload of flour, the situation might have been different.

As soon as the vehicles entered Rafah itself, I saw the changes around us. Warfare was clearly underway. Despite the pledged Israeli assault on Rafah not having started, there were certainly a number of destroyed buildings from targeted missile attacks, and many temporary shelters on the pavements, shelters that were home to Internally Displaced Persons (IDPs). Not every shelter belonged to an IDP. Most did, but there were a few where the richer and more fortunate families had decided to leave their houses and live instead in a shelter. That way they would not stand out from the rest.

Despite aid being donated, and thus officially free to a recipient, in Gaza that was not always the case. The young men with wooden clubs at the Rafah crossing highlighted that. On many street corners I saw tables loaded with small quantities of food. This was aid food that had reached the Black Market and was being sold rather than donated. If there was a way of making money in a zone of conflict, someone was bound to find it, whether the moneymaking exercise was honest or dishonest. The rules of survival in a war zone were different to those outside. Standards changed, behaviours changed, once the primary aim of existence became survival. Criminality was almost normal.

There was a huge rate of war-related inflation in Gaza, estimated to be 37 per cent, and some items were impossible to find. As we drove through the centre of Rafah city, I saw a single ATM in action, and a line of people waiting for it that stretched for over 100 metres. It was the only ATM functioning in Rafah. There was dirt almost anywhere I looked, while the traffic was slow, dense, and unpredictable. There were no traffic lights, indicators appeared not to be used even if they were functional, and when horns were honked, they were pressed hard and with anger.

At one point the traffic became even denser, and I watched a convoy of several ambulances pass by, going in the opposite direction. They carried the sad and destroyed bodies of the seven aid workers from World Central Kitchen who had been killed the day before near Deir-al-Balah. There was much media activity around them, plenty of body armour emblazoned with "Press" to see, the occasional helmet although not many, as each journalist desperately tried to pen a story. Where was I going? Deir-al-Balah, of course. I could have done without seeing the ambulances.

Immediately before our arrival, there had been a surge of military attacks across different areas near Deir-al-Balah city, which was where we would shortly be headed. Israeli soldiers had targeted a residential house in the city, killing at least four Palestinians. I do not know why. The targeting formed part of the ongoing destruction of residential homes in the southern part of Gaza, the city of Khan Yunis also being hit. Since the early hours of that morning, there had been loud explosions from Khan Yunis, with palls of smoke rising on the horizon. There were serious confrontations underway and battles still ongoing. Barely ten of Gaza's 36 hospitals were now functioning, a number that was diminishing. Even those where medical work was feasible, were barely able to cope.

After 30 minutes of slow driving, sometimes even being stationary, we arrived at MAP's Rafah headquarters. There, I had the chance to talk in depth to the local staff in Rafah. I knew worry when I saw it, and in their eyes and body language I saw plenty. Each time there was another crump or thump, I saw their glances, as they tried to work out if the fighting was coming nearer or was still a few kilometres away. Israel had declared that it wished to invade Rafah, an event for which all were preparing. Consequently, each crump or thump might have meant the fighting was getting closer. Few wished to be in Rafah when the Israelis arrived.

Everything was near to everything in Gaza. Distances that would seem too near in other parts of the world, were seen as massive in the territory. We were scheduled to be going to Al Aqsa Hospital in Deir-al-Balah the following morning, a distance of barely 20.8 kilometres (12.9 miles). However, judged by the increased crumps and thumps coming from that direction, it seemed there was an increased risk of attack, so we discussed whether we should move to another hospital. One option was the European General Hospital (EGH) in Khan Yunis. Sadly, even that was being targeted. It was also a popular location for foreign medical teams to work and at times EGH had more medics than it knew how to handle. It was a strong reason why we preferred to work at Al Aqsa, not EGH, so despite the crumps and thumps we decided we would still head to Deir-al-Balah.

Dinner in Rafah was exceptional, especially when considering the war. Based on rice, which summed up most dishes in Gaza, the meal was *maqloubeh*. The word meant "upside down" in Arabic and was a traditional Levantine dish that the local staff had prepared for us, as a welcome to our new home. *Maqloubeh* was so well-known that it had even featured in the Israeli-Palestinian conflict. There had once been an attempt to label the dish as Israeli, but the Palestinians complained and stated it was evidence of cultural appropriation. *Maqloubeh* had also been used by Palestinian activists to encourage people to join protests at the Aqsa Mosque in occupied East Jerusalem. The dish traditionally included various vegetables, such as fried tomato, potato, cauliflower, and eggplant, accompanied by either chicken or lamb. However, in Rafah, assorted vegetables were in short supply thanks to the war. In our case it was chicken, as there was no chance of finding lamb.

The ingredients of a *maqloubeh* are carefully placed in the pot in layers, so when the pot is inverted for serving, the dish looks like a layer cake. In Rafah, we missed out on the inversion and just tucked in. It did not take long for the bowl to be emptied as everyone was enormously hungry. It had been a very long day.

Palestine had a strong connection with food, not just *maqloubeh*. In happier times, there were many local dishes – *zibdieh*, *sumaghiyyeh*, *qidra*, and others. To have even tried an uninverted *maqloubeh* in the middle of a war, and with famine on the horizon, was remarkable. Definitely an occasion to remember.

With instructions to be ready to move by 8:00 a.m. in the morning, I felt myself dozing, so headed for bed, which was actually a sleeping bag on a mattress. I took a shower beforehand, which would normally have been lengthy but water was in short supply and anyway was cold. I darted this way and that, breathed in and out irregularly, tried not to be noisy, washed myself as best I could, also washed a few clothes as I showered, and was soon in my sleeping bag waiting for sleep to take hold. In the distance I heard shells and missiles falling and what sounded to be a heavy machine gun. There was no purpose in worrying as these were sounds I would be hearing continually during my time in Gaza. What was certain was that with our journey to Deir-al-Balah in the morning we would be going towards the fighting, not away. Tomorrow would be more perilous than today.

Within minutes I was snoring, at least according to my room mates who arrived a little later. The one good thing about snoring is that the snorer is never troubled. It is only those around who are kept awake.

\* \* \*

# Chapter 6

# Arriving at Al Aqsa

As an early riser, I was up at 5:30 a.m. after a remarkably decent sleep, considering I was slumbering in a war zone. I left my two room companions snoozing – they were well in the Land of Nod. The few clothes I had washed before going to my bed were predictably still wet. I had not been doing well with drying clothes on the mission and remembered my soggy socks in Cairo. So once again, on went the soggy socks plus a soggy T-shirt, the way of things it seemed when involved with Gaza.

Overhead, I could hear the buzz of drones, the locals called them *zinnanah* after the buzz of a mosquito. There was also distant shellfire, or perhaps missiles exploding, sounds that were coming from my north.

It seemed I had odd thoughts in the mornings I pondered, as I chuckled to myself quietly. I must contact the IDF, I decided unrealistically, and ask them to confine bombing to daylight hours only so that others could sleep. Somehow, I suspected they would not listen.

Slowly everyone awakened but there were two who were not feeling well. One was coughing and spluttering, which was a risk of infection for the rest of us. In addition, it would not look good to the locals if foreign medics arrived and spread disease. The other had a gut that was misbehaving. It seemed best if both stayed in Rafah until they were better, while the remainder headed for Al Aqsa and began their duties right away. It was important to be fit, as aid worker casualties in Gaza were mounting and the territory was known to be the most dangerous place in the world to be a humanitarian. Sometimes an aid worker had to move quickly, there was no predicting when, so fitness was a prerequisite.

The most dangerous part of any war zone was when travelling from one point to another. Once in a fixed location, there was clearly risk, but in transit this increased hugely. From Rafah we would be heading directly towards the sounds of battle and there was no denying the gamble.

The deaths of the seven aid workers belonging to World Central Kitchen (WCK) had created huge issues in the humanitarian sector and lay heavily on our minds, even if we outwardly pretended to ignore it. Our route to Al Aqsa Hospital went straight past the location where they had been killed. WCK had become well established and well respected in the humanitarian sector since it had first been founded by the Michelin-starred chef José Andrés in 2010. It had already suspended its operations in Gaza after the attack. WCK was funded via individual donations, foundations, and public charities, and had operated in more than 45 countries. It was not a small player, so we had to pay attention to what had happened. There was no guarantee that the same would not happen to us. It appeared that Israel was sending a message. Aid workers were not welcome.

Other organisations had acted in different ways, but mostly with caution. The UN had cancelled night-time operations, the UAE had stopped all activities completely, as had an organisation called Anera, which had been working alongside WCK. It had lost a volunteer one month earlier thanks to an airstrike. The Gaza conflict had caused almost three times the death toll of humanitarian workers recorded in any single conflict within a year, wherever in the world. Even ambulance convoys had been attacked on multiple occasions. Affected organisations had included the Palestinian Red Crescent, the International Committee of the Red Cross (ICRC), Médecins Sans Frontières (MSF), the United Nations Relief and Works Agency (UNRWA), and many others. The UN Secretary General, António Guterres, summarised the situation well when he had first described the problem in December 2023:

> *"136 of our colleagues in Gaza have been killed in 75 days – something we have never seen in the history of the United Nations. Nowhere is safe in Gaza."*

He was right. There was nowhere safe in Gaza. Although it might have appeared more secure to have cancelled or postponed our mission to Al Aqsa Hospital in the wake of the WCK attack, now we were en route it seemed sensible to keep going. My analogy was that it was like an avalanche. When an avalanche slid down a slope of snow, it left behind an area of reasonable stability. That would not last long but for a few days it was possible to ski across the slope, until more snow accumulated. In an odd way, the same could be said of the WCK attack. The worldwide outcry after the killings, some would even say murders, probably meant we would be safer travelling than staying put. To travel north seemed a fair bet. It was not the time to avoid the area and to my astonishment everyone agreed.

The war appeared to be picking up pace and not reaching any real conclusion. Israel seemed to be finding everything extremely hard work, however optimistic the global news was trying to appear. It seemed that the Hamas tunnel network was far larger than Israel expected, and Hamas was only feeling slight pressure. The conflict could keep going for a very long time and throughout, humanitarian work had to continue.

Israel had called up air defence reservists thanks to their missile attack on the Iranian consulate in Syria's Damascus, even if Israel never claimed responsibility. In Gaza itself, four properties were attacked by the IDF last night, in addition to further attacks on IDP camps. The situation in Gaza was becoming more dire by the moment. The UN had said that about 1.7 million people, or 75 per cent of the population, had been displaced since 7 October 2023, with more than one million of those IDPs being in Rafah. Displacement was frequently multiple. When a Palestinian was forced to move, they might have to move again, and again, and again, as the war proceeded. In my discussions with many locals, to find those who had moved at least six times, once their primary home had been reduced to rubble, was extremely common. There was one individual I met who had moved 13 times in six months. There was no central organisation that handled the displacements. All an IDP did was to leave home and set up camp anywhere that seemed sensible.

Meanwhile children were dying of starvation in northern Gaza, famine was imminent and likely to occur throughout the territory within the next few weeks. This was certainly not helped by episodes such as the WCK tragedy. Residents of northern Gaza had been forced to survive on an average of 245 calories per day since January. Compare that with the 2,500 calories per day that would normally be seen in the UK. Meanwhile, more than 60 per cent of housing units had been destroyed, along with 392 education facilities, 123 ambulances and 184 mosques. These were very significant numbers.

It was barely a 21-kilometre drive from Rafah in South Gaza to Deir-al-Balah in Central Gaza. However, as a journey it could take between 45 minutes and two hours, as there were many hazards on

There was more damage in Gaza than in Dresden during the Second World War.

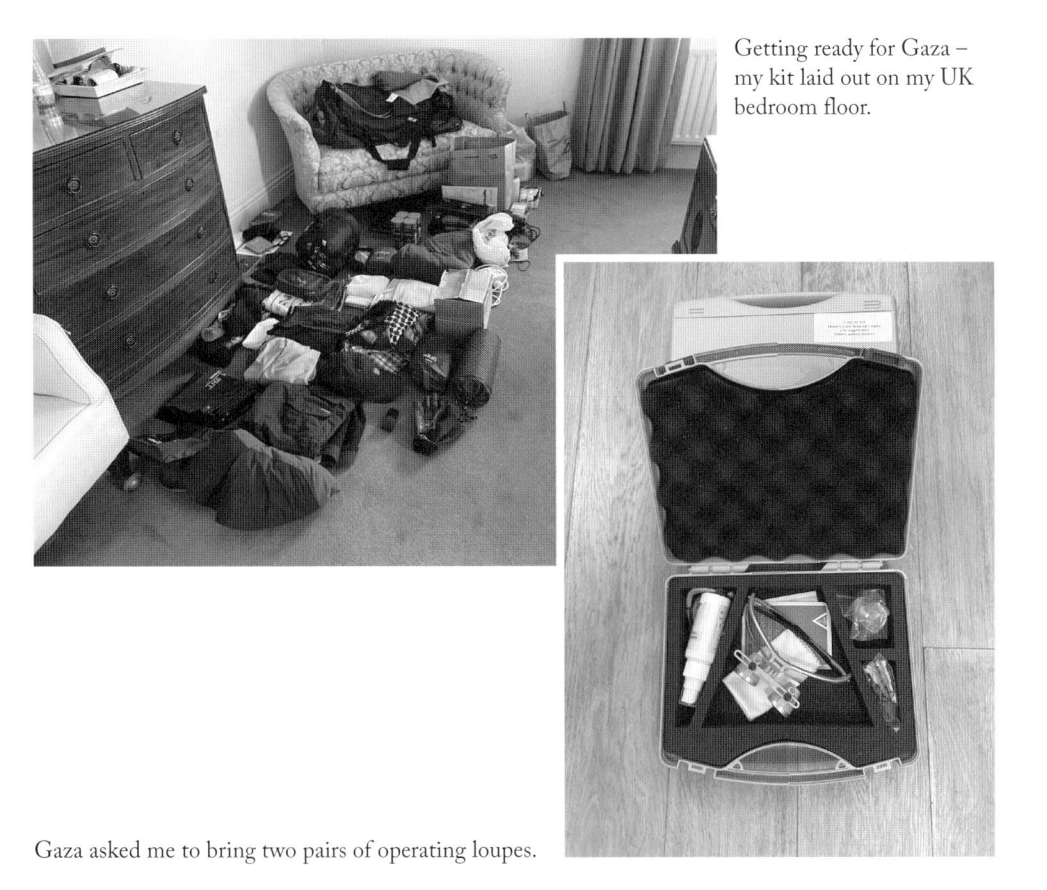

Getting ready for Gaza – my kit laid out on my UK bedroom floor.

Gaza asked me to bring two pairs of operating loupes.

The team began to assemble at London Heathrow Airport.

Training to apply a tourniquet.

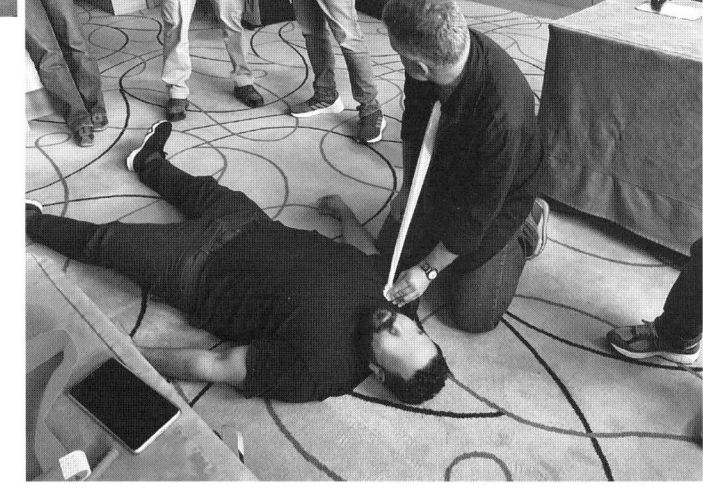

Training to plug a sucking chest wound.

Briefing for the much-depleted convoy across the Sinai Peninsula.

Aid lorries parked and waiting to enter Gaza.

You need to stay healthy so be careful with the water.

Looking up Arish beach towards Gaza.

Israeli missiles killed seven World Central Kitchen workers very nearly simultaneously.

The huge expanse of the Sinai Peninsula, which had to be crossed to reach Gaza.

The Sinai Peninsula was a Bedouin area.

IDP tents on the streets of Rafah.

Child eking out a living while adults look at posters which explain what aid they will receive.

Attempting to keep life normal.

Trying hard with agriculture in Gaza.

UNRWA undertook some very impressive work.

The devastation was indescribable. (*Photograph by Emad El Byed on Unsplash*)

More than 10,000 bodies are said to lie under Gaza's rubble. (*Photograph by Emad El Byed on Unsplash*)

the way. First, and essential, was the so-called deconfliction from the Israelis, which theoretically permitted travel without hazard. Sadly, the WCK incident had shown otherwise so even with deconfliction established, one still had to hope. Although we were deconflicted for the journey between Rafah and Al Aqsa, I still spent much of the journey looking nervously at the sky. Throughout the trip, there were intermittent, billowing explosions 500 metres to my right while *zinnanah* buzzed overhead.

Much of the drive to Deir-al-Balah, and the Al Aqsa Hospital where I would be working, was slow and snail-like. The road was largely pitted dirt-track, weaving its way northwards along the coast through extensive tented encampments, with occasional stretches of smooth tarmac to gather my hopes. These stretches did not last long. On my left was a glorious Mediterranean, flat and glistening. An Israeli warship remained on the far horizon, to remind me that the pancake sea was also a no-go area. If it was not for the war, Gaza would be a perfect holiday destination. Since antiquity it had been a prosperous oasis and a commercial hub that served as a springboard for any Middle Eastern empire to conquer Egypt and for any Nile Valley-based power to attack the Levant. Sadly, none of that was possible today but despite the fighting and distrust, plenty of the original Gaza remained.

Apart from Gaza's once scenic nature, much of the route to Deir-al-Balah was lined either side by improvised, tented homes for IDPs. Each tented area had done its best to make something from nothing. The war had turned this Palestinian territory upside down. Most life now took place outdoors, there was evident paucity of food, and every form of transport imaginable could be seen. There were locals in fossil-fuel-powered vehicles, not many, but also walking, on bicycles, or travelling by donkey, or even camel, and cart.

At one point where the dirt-track road narrowed, we had to slow down. There was plenty of slowing in Gaza. To reach 20 kilometres/hour was a record. Mostly we were crawling at 5 kilometres/hour or less. As we slowed for the road, it so happened that a fully laden lorry was coming in the opposite direction. I believe it was filled with aid. Suddenly, and without any warning, a young boy who was barely 8 years old, dashed across the road in front of us. We performed an emergency stop and missed him, although not by far, but the young boy carried on. Within moments he was under the lorry opposite us, and I was certain I would see a crushed head any moment. Yet that was not to be. The boy's reflexes were swift, and he ducked, twisted, and shoved. Somehow, he wriggled clear without major injury, although he did knock his head in the process. The boy's Maker had clearly intervened, and the child walked free. Remarkable.

When I saw the boy rub his injured head, and although it was not bleeding, the doctor in me wanted to get out of the car and help. I tried the door handle but found it locked.

"Please unlock my door," I half shouted to the driver.

Instantly I saw Security, who was sitting in the front passenger seat, turn towards me.

"Why?" he asked.

"I need to help that young boy," I answered, pointing at the child through my closed but chipped rear car window.

"You do not," said Security. "Stay exactly where you are. You will not get out of this car for any reason."

He was right, of course. For me to emerge from the car would attract attention. That was the last thing we needed, especially with the WCK tragedy having taken place nearby. We were barely one kilometre from where the first missile had struck.

It so happened that through the car window I could see the boy recovering so that all I would probably have done is hold a distressed hand. I thus muttered something approaching agreement, and the car lurched onward, the young boy slowly becoming a dot in the rear view mirror. He would never have known of my existence.

I had barely recovered from the shock of seeing the child being nearly squashed, when 300 metres further on, again we were travelling at a snail-like pace, beside the road I saw a near-naked elderly man being attacked by a middle-aged man, who was thumping him hard with a wooden stick. Two other middle-aged men were holding the elderly man down. The victim was alive, although barely so, and trying futilely to protect his head and face from the forceful wooden blows.

"What's happening here?" I asked Security, who was sitting in the front passenger seat. It is called the bullet-catcher seat when in a war zone and I always choose to sit behind it if I can. The aim is that any bullet entering the windscreen will first strike the bullet-catcher and then their seat. With luck the bullet will be stopped and not travel so far as to strike anyone in the back. The fatter the person in the bullet-catcher seat, the greater the chance of survival in the back. Sadly, Security in Gaza was thin.

"He's being punished for selling aid," Security replied.

The elderly man being clubbed had stolen some aid, only six tins of tomatoes, and had tried selling them on the roadside. Much of what I saw on the tables lining each side of the road was stolen aid, likely hijacked near the Rafah crossing. We had almost been hijacked there ourselves. The elderly man had done what so many others tried to do but had been caught and was paying the penalty. He would be clubbed vigorously but would not be killed. It would then be his choice if he chose to sell aid again. The next clubbing would be harder. I imagined he would eventually be clubbed to death if he kept on going. Once again, I was not permitted to help, although I doubt there was much I could have done anyway.

Each side of us as we drove were multiple queues of Gazans waiting for various distributions of aid, water in particular. They were mainly waiting patiently, certainly at the tail end of a queue, but as they drew closer to the water distribution point itself, discernible by two large white water tanks, the hustling and jostling began. All around and nearby were puddles of raw sewage. Thanks to the ordering of a complete siege of Gaza by Israel, clean water was unavailable for most living in the territory. Israeli airstrikes were destroying water infrastructure and wells in possible violation of international humanitarian law. During times of conflict, international humanitarian law prohibited the attacking or destroying of what were described as "objects indispensable to the survival of the civilian population." Water infrastructure and drinking water installations came under this heading

Even before the current crisis, Gazans struggled to access adequate safe water. About 90 per cent of Gaza's water supply came from the Coastal Aquifer Basin, which ran along the eastern Mediterranean coast from Egypt through Gaza and into Israel. However, the water was brackish and contaminated because of seawater intrusion, overextraction, sewage, and chemical infiltration. Consequently, Gazans relied on small-scale desalination units and unregulated private water tankers, which could be costly and were not always pure. The remaining 10 per cent of water not pumped from the Coastal Aquifer Basin came primarily from three Israeli pipelines and from small-scale seawater desalination plants. As a result of Israel's siege, Gazans' access to water from all sources, including desalination and external Israeli sources, quickly dropped by 95 per cent after the beginning of the war.

It took about 90 minutes to eventually reach Deir-al-Balah's Al Aqsa Martyrs Hospital, which was busier than busy. Our route had taken us directly past the point where the WCK convoy had been attacked, very near to the hospital, although the vehicles had since been removed. The hospital courtyard and grounds around were filled with Gazans who had fled from the fighting and who felt a hospital was a safer place to stay than setting up a temporary home outside. That said, an Israeli air strike had hit the tented camp in the courtyard of the hospital four days earlier, the claim being that four members of Islamic Jihad (IJ) were being targeted. I had no idea if that was true, but the site of the attack was perilously close to the hospital. It was either thanks to incredible accuracy by Israel, or good luck, that many more people were not injured.

Within 30 minutes of arrival at Al Aqsa Hospital, I was at work. A brief word with the Head of Nursing was all it required and then away I went. The hospital was packed to busting, similar perhaps to the feeling I sometimes had in London during the rush-hour crush on the London underground.

The hospital, which was formerly the main maternity unit for the area, normally had 200 beds but had increased its capacity to at least 700. It would be wrong to say beds, as many of the patients were on mattresses on the floor, lying in corridors, or even on the stairs outside. There were patients just about everywhere I went. In addition, there were 3,000 IDPs camped outside. These numbers were a guesstimate as in reality they felt considerably larger. The hospital also originally had two operating theatres but had redesigned things so that it had five. To make this possible, it had converted three maternity delivery suites into small operating theatres. There was nothing special about these temporary operating theatres. Essentially they were glorified consultation rooms and carried no special equipment. They were largely for simple or infected cases, but surgery of any sort could take place there if there happened to be a mass casualty incident underway.

There were patients and plastic tents in corridors, and new emergencies were being admitted continually. I am an orthopaedic surgeon, that is bones and joints, and for this specialty at Al Aqsa there were three teams, each on duty for 12 hours, and doing turn and turnabout.

I focussed first on the wards, as there were so many patients, few ward staff, and it was easy for critical issues to be missed. For example, a patient might become short of breath several days after an operation, a possible indicator of a blood clot on the lung, and which could be life threatening. It would need speedy action but only if there was sufficient attendance by ward staff to pick it up. Or a vascular operation could be undertaken expertly but perhaps a stitch (*suture*) might slip several days later. The next thing was for the patient to suddenly start bleeding, or for the limb to turn blue and die. Or a wound might become infected, an extremely common occurrence at Al Aqsa. If identified early then antibiotics, if available might be all that was needed to settle the problem. If the infection was identified late in the day, antibiotics might be insufficient and further surgery needed. Again, such things could be avoided if identified early. Good ward care was critical for a hospital like Al Aqsa and yet seemed to be lacking.

It was difficult to say what was ward and what was corridor, as there were patients almost everywhere I looked. I weaved my way through the swarm of casualties – it really was a swarm – to find just a few that were troubling the locals. I could see why. There was so much work taking place in the operating theatres that once a patient made it back to the ward after surgery, it was easy for them to be lost, ignored, or both. Postoperative complications could occur without anyone knowing. Chronic bone infection was common and many of the amputation stumps were so infected they could not be stitched closed and had to be left open to heal over time, if they would heal at all.

Patients who had undergone surgery were receiving little postoperative care and there was an extreme shortage of physiotherapists, wheelchairs, and splints. Just about anything that would be an expected normal in most other parts of the world was lacking at Al Aqsa. Each patient I saw was the victim of a blast injury, other than one, who had sustained a gunshot wound. This was real war surgery and there was no avoiding it.

What was also evident was the toughness of the Palestinians. These people were extraordinarily strong. This was well exemplified by one patient who had broken (fractured) his left elbow three weeks earlier and a surgeon had externally fixed the break. This means that pins had been inserted into the bone, were left protruding while the protruding ends were fixed together with a stiff metal bar. It is one method of immobilising a fracture so that the thing can heal. The principle of external fixation is to have as little penetrating the skin as possible, thereby reducing the chances of infection, while also allowing the skin and soft tissues to remain exposed so that a wound can be watched and dressed.

External fixation is the opposite of internal fixation. When a fracture is internally fixed, a metal fixation device, perhaps a rod down the middle of a bone, or screws and plates fixed to the side of a bone, are used. Such fixation devices may offer rigid fixation of a fracture and greater security than external fixation, but there can be a higher chance of infection creeping in. Once bone is infected, the patient has great problems, as curing infected bone is a big problem. In medical language, infected bone is called *osteomyelitis*. Even if a fractured bone is tightly fixed, be that with external or internal fixation, the bone still must heal. Any fixation will only last for a limited period, its main task being to hold the bone in position while it heals. Osteomyelitis, that is infected bone, delays or totally prevents healing and leads to what doctors call an *infected non-union*. There are many of those in war zones, far too many in fact. Al Aqsa showed plenty.

For the Palestinian with an external fixation device positioned close to his left elbow, one might imagine it would be too painful for the elbow to move. Not for him. I asked the patient to bend and straighten an elbow that had not moved since surgery, three weeks earlier. Quick as a flash he did so, bending and straightening the elbow with near ease, without his face showing a flicker of discomfort. Remarkable. Thankfully, his X-rays showed no signs of infected non-union, although in practice it can take several months for bone infection to become visible on an X-ray.

As I visited these various complex patients, I found that most of the Palestinians thought the world had dismissed them and they were alone. One very common question was, "Why has the world forgotten us? What does everyone outside think of what is going on here?"

I was surprised to hear this, as there was plenty of opposition to the war taking place in my country, and around the world as well. It appeared there was a news blackout taking place in Gaza, an attempt to make the Palestinians feel isolated.

I reassured them they were wrong, and I could see they were happy to hear that. Irrespective of what many governments were saying, and how each country might have been trying to manipulate public opinion, in my own UK I had regularly found friends and colleagues who were appalled at what was taking place before the world's eyes in Gaza. I found very few who supported it, if any at all.

I listened to the persistent crump and thump of shells and missiles exploding not far away, as yet another batch of civilian casualties was admitted from the street. The stream of ambulance sirens was largely continuous, while so many of the patients I saw around me were children, women, and the elderly. The number of young adult males was tiny. I was no lawyer, and was grateful to be a doctor, as the legalities of what I saw were questionable. It was simpler just to focus on the patients, as that way I would not have to judge if a war crime was underway. There were hazards to being medical in a war zone, but there were advantages as well.

The hospital provided the tiniest of accommodations, with one room being provided for us all, a team of six adults. One glance showed that it would barely be feasible to have three people sleeping there, certainly not the six we had, or even five if our one lady slept elsewhere. There was one bed available, and the rest would have mattresses on the floor.

Directly outside the tiny accommodation was a hospital corridor that had been converted into a ward, so patients were immediately nearby and would disturb us regularly, knocking on the door to seek advice. Security insisted that we reposition the mattresses so that we were less at risk from flying glass fragments, in the event a missile landed nearby. There was fragmentation film on the glass windows, essentially this was clear sticky-backed plastic, and two windows were left slightly open to equalise external and internal pressures in the case of any blast. The team had also been allocated a washroom, although this contained only a handheld shower and no bath, was two corridors away, and was shared with the ladies.

I decided this arrangement was not for me, so after this first night in hospital accommodation I would travel daily from Rafah to Deir-al-Balah, even if the journey was lengthy. It would be the best way of seeing the true effects of war on a formidable but struggling population. To have a clearer idea of the patients in the hospital, I had also to see them outside. The only way of doing so would be to drive through their tented camps daily. It would mean a daily return road journey between

Rafah and Deir-al-Balah, with all the dangers and problems that might ensue, but I could think of no better way of seeing Gaza at war.

That evening, and after a day of hard work, a delayed dinner was eventually served of rice, meat, and dates. We ate it on the floor of our tiny accommodation on disposable plates and used a sheet as a tablecloth. We were so busy eating that no one spoke, until a *zinnanah* flew overhead in the darkness. Its buzz was unmistakeable, and we thought it might be sizing us up for a strike.

"Here we go," said one.

"Wait for it," said another.

"That must mean something," said a third.

No sooner had the *zinnanah* flown by, than a shoot-out with semi-automatic weapons began in the hospital grounds, just outside our window and only metres from where we were eating. Shoot-outs are very noisy, especially when they are nearby, and in a built-up area, but this one ended without casualties. I never did establish why the shoot-out had occurred although was later told they were warning shots, largely in the air, and Palestinian-on-Palestinian. Meanwhile the *zinnanah* came and went and we had a night without missiles, but only the night. Early the next day, the crumps and thumps returned, as did the *zinnanah*.

* * *

Chapter 7

# When Palestinians Worry

I was astonished to find that Al Aqsa Hospital had a dawn chorus. Largely house sparrows and doves, but there were still birds to hear, which I found incredible for a war zone. Normally, when I teach others about war surgery, I say that, in war, the birds disappear. Not at Al Aqsa, it seemed.

I awoke after a disturbed night thanks to two team colleagues who were observing the Ramadan fast, and who arose to eat their *suhoor* in the pre-dawn hours. The *suhoor* is the Ramadan pre-dawn meal. I listened to them munching, not the most pleasant sound in the early morning hours, and then I drifted back to sleep. I woke two hours later, to an air that was alive with birdsong. I was astonished. But added to the birdsong were other sounds, too. There was the buzz of an overhead *zinnanah* that circled and recircled the hospital, no more than 1,000 feet overhead. I imagined spotty adolescents in Tel Aviv becoming bored as they went round and round the same spot, wondering what to bomb next, and fitting in more human tragedy before slipping off unnoticed to take breakfast. The callousness of modern war. Although the bombing might make another human family homeless, widowed, motherless, childless, or maimed, the birds were made homeless, too. So many had made their homes in the eaves of buildings. When the IDF flattened a building, human tragedy was one consequence, but animal tragedy occurred as well.

The birds stopped their tweeting immediately after an explosion or the sound of gunfire, but only when it was nearby. When the sounds of war were in the distance, as they were when I heard them from my mattress, the birds had long ceased caring and continued their darting, diving flight, tweeting all the while. I was listening to the dawn chorus of war – birds, *zinnanah*, distant shells, missiles, and heavy machine-gun fire. A far cry from London.

The humans, too, knew when to worry or relax. Despite me being ex-military, I sometimes found it hard to distinguish the various noises of war. I have mistaken someone hammering a metal panel for gunfire, a slamming door for a grenade, while the hospital floor above me had a cavity wall, which sounded like a bomb when people leaned on it. There was a rumble, which I could both hear and feel, exactly like a distant explosion. I cannot understand why.

The Palestinians, and to me they were stronger than oxen, looked at me with sympathy. "Can't you tell?" they asked, "that is not an explosion. It is a rumbling wall."

"You are the experts," I said, and together we laughed.

"We will tell you when to worry," they continued. "Until then just carry on."

They were right. All I then did was watch Palestinians. When they ducked, I did. When they relaxed, so did I.

Islam teaches its followers to understand death. Some even welcome it. Mohammad, our Jordanian theatre nurse, put it succinctly by quoting the Quran:

*"But never will Allah delay a soul when its time has come."*

Islam had a point. So I chose to carry on regardless, unflinching, and trusted that today would not be the day. Yet if it was, so be it.

As well as the birds, there were flowers, too, despite all that was happening. Not many, but a few. Somehow a bright red hibiscus had escaped the foragers, so Nature was doing what she could to survive while mankind continued onwards crazily. It surprised me that the hibiscus was untouched, as it could be a more than useful plant. Parts of the flower could make a popular Egyptian drink called *karkade* while it also had medicinal uses when treating colds, heart and nerve diseases, and even as a gentle laxative. It had many other uses, too. Hibiscus was both a chef's and medic's dream, yet Al Aqsa Hospital had left one untouched. I could not explain why.

My day started with another ward round, and first to a family that had been decimated in an explosion two days earlier. All the patients I had seen so far had been civilian, and this family was no exception. Women, children, and the elderly were the rule rather than exception. The decimated family was in a terrible state and made me feel that my Arabic should be better. It was an occasion when I wanted to sit beside the patient, hold their hand – difficult in Islamic society – look into their eyes and empathise. I could not speak the language sufficiently well to do so, sadly.

The family's story once again brought a tear to my otherwise hardened eye. The mother had sustained an open fracture of her right shin bone (tibia) and had an external fixator in place. Her 4-year-old son had been killed while her young baby had survived. Her husband, who was in his fifties, had sustained a fracture of his thighbone (femur) and was in a bed in the hospital corridor outside the room occupied by his wife. How the family could handle its bereavement, in addition to their major injuries when they had nothing to do with the conflict upset me, and I had to step away for a breather. There were few places to hide in Al Aqsa, so I found a remote corridor and stood alone in some half-darkness for a while, regathering my strength and emotions. These were unnecessary casualties in an unnecessary war. The reasons why they were wounded and bereaved escaped me. I had to hope that whoever had their finger on the button, which had led to this complex of injuries and death, truly believed in what they were doing and was not mindlessly following orders. If the latter, let them hang their head in shame. A family had been tragically torn apart for no reason.

Six months into the war, more than 13,800 children had been killed and more than 12,009 injured in Gaza. The figures for the West Bank were 113 and 725 for the same, respectively. At least 50 per cent of the injured were children aged less than 10 years. The word "injury" did not truly cover what was happening. It would be better to say "wounded". Because these were largely wounds created by explosions, they were multiple. It was unusual to receive a casualty with a single wound. It was the number of wounds that counted, not so much the number of casualties. Each wound needed its own operation, and each could lead to infection and disability. Amputation was more common in this war. There was a time when it was unusual to amputate a Palestinian's limb but now it seemed more usual. How I remember the Great March of Return in 2018 when I saw more than 400 casualties but did not perform a single amputation. How Gaza had changed. Children were amputees as well. The United Nations Children's Fund (UNICEF) reported that at least 1,000 children had required one or both legs to be amputated since the beginning of the war. That was six Gazan children becoming amputees daily, and in a territory where there was no one available to make an artificial limb. Appalling. Two Gazan mothers were also killed every hour. The death toll for women and children in Gaza was more than six times that of the ongoing Russia-Ukraine War, if ever a comparator was needed.

As I walked the wards of Al Aqsa Hospital, I soon realised how sparse was their equipment, and how inexperienced their staff. There were midwives caring for war injuries and not being paid. The place was shored up by unpaid volunteers, some with little or no clinical experience and no knowledge of sterile techniques. I knew that some equipment had been donated by various organisations, not huge amounts, but at least some. There were items that the wards would say were needed for their patients, yet they had no clue if those items were already available or whether they should start the ordering process right away. Ordering equipment for a Gaza hospital needed luck and perseverance and could take a very long time. I thus thought to visit the hospital's stores. Might it be that the stores contained more than was thought? The only way of finding out was to check.

"Where are the stores?" I asked.

"In the basement," said a fellow surgeon, indicating downwards with his thumb. Together we paid a visit to the underground stores, to see what might already have been donated.

The place was chaos. Large quantities of equipment and disposable items that had been donated from throughout the world had been piled erratically in the stores. The locals who worked there appeared to have scant idea of what had been received and little record had been made.

"What do you need?" I asked one storeman.

"Lots of beds," came the reply, which I could understand.

A new unit was being speedily constructed to house the overflow of patients. Had it been my UK National Health Service, a new building would have taken months or years to construct. This was war-torn Gaza, so from idea to full construction had taken barely ten days.

I nodded to the storeman and walked briefly around the stores. As I did so, I passed at least 20 beds that had been donated but about which the storeman had no idea. Immediately above them, on an otherwise overloaded and higgledy-piggledy shelf, were dozens of crutches. A physiotherapist, one of only five available for the entire hospital, had only just asked me for more crutches.

"We have none," she had declared, unaware of what already lay in the hospital's stores.

Rehabilitation after many of the war wounds I had so far seen was a critical part of recovery. If a patient received ten minutes of physiotherapy once each week at Al Aqsa, they were doing well. Because of this, many of the injured had stiff knees, immobile fingers, fixed elbows, frozen shoulders, and more. Physiotherapy was an essential part of recovery. Back home in the UK, I used it for most of my patients. Physiotherapists, to me, were the unsung heroes of healthcare.

The physiotherapist was unaware that several floors under her feet, lying in a tangled basement, were many of the crutches she sought. Not all, but some. It was a feature of war hospitals. There was so much going on that the left hand frequently did not know what the right hand was doing. Pressure of work simply prevented it. I was unsure how one might be better organised when there was a *zinnanah* buzzing overhead and shells and missiles were falling. Perhaps it was a peril of war.

Restrictions on the access of aid to Gaza added to these troubles. I had already seen the long lines of trucks each side of the road, waiting to enter the territory. There were stationary trucks on the roadsides as far back as Cairo, 320 kilometres away. All aid had first to be approved by Israel before it was permitted to enter Gaza. If a single item was rejected, and sometimes there was no apparent logic in the rejection, certainly no reasons were given, so a full lorryload could be declined and would turn for home. The list of forbidden items varied from day to day and month to month and made little sense – solar panels, generators, water purification tablets, X-ray machines, ventilators, anaesthetic agents, filtration systems, oxygen cylinders, tent poles and, of course, crutches. Doubtless, one day someone might explain.

A problem of there being so many patients was that it was simple to miss things, especially when there were multiple wounds created by an explosive device. Patients were checked on admission, but once they reached the ward, so the care became less detailed. It was simply the effect of numbers. One patient in his mid-fifties worried me especially, as he had been admitted with shrapnel injuries to the back of his left thigh, had lost the little finger of his right hand when putting up his hand to protect his head from falling debris, and had multiple small shrapnel puncture wounds to his right shin bone. This had all happened three weeks before I had entered Gaza and a single missile had done the lot.

"My right ankle feels strange," he said. He could not explain how, but the description was the best he could do.

I examined the patient's ankle and instantly thought that the joint had been broken, not just in one place but two. As no X-ray had been taken of the ankle when the patient had first arrived in the Emergency Department three weeks earlier, I asked for an X-ray to double-check what I thought. When I returned to see the X-ray one hour later, it seemed clear I had been right. The ankle had been broken in two places when he had first been admitted three weeks earlier, yet the injury had been missed all along, so distracted had the staff been by the patient's other injuries. Missing an injury is easily done and happens commonly in war zones. Less so in peaceful UK but frequently in Gaza. I then had to think what to do.

X-rays are common items that most people would recognise but at Al Aqsa Hospital there were no viewing screens on the wards, nor for patients in the corridors. The patient with the broken ankle was in a corridor like so many others. However, the patients were wise to this so always took a photograph of the X-ray image on their mobile telephone when the X-ray was done. Every Palestinian I met in Gaza was the owner of a mobile telephone. All I needed do was ask to see an X-ray and the patient would instantly show me the image on their mobile. Despite the war horrors around me, this system worked well, and I never once lost an X-ray.

Having identified the fractures for the first time three weeks after the patient's admission, I decided it would be best to internally fix the fractured ankle. That is, insert metalwork to hold the fractures together. However, I would have to be careful as the various shrapnel wounds affecting the patient were slowly becoming infected. I did not wish any metalwork I inserted to become infected as well. I thus made sure the patient was given a high dose of antibiotics and I then did a limited fixation, using a single screw rather than a screw plus screws and plate. Instead of the screws and plate I used a plaster cast, and all went well. My principle was based on the fact that I needed metalwoerk to stabilise the fracture, yet the more metalwork I put in, so the chances of infection would rise. I tried to strike a happy medium and felt that I did. War surgery is a continual balancing act. A particular fracture or wound might ideally be treated in a certain way, but circumstance and lack of equipment indicate something different. The patient showed this perfectly. I had to adapt what I did to the circumstances before me.

The operation was not difficult but there were many problems with the operating theatre routine that one would never wish to see in a normal hospital. It was likely that the pressures of war had encouraged corners to be cut. For example, the leg on which I was operating had not been marked with a black felt pen, something that was routine in normal practice to reduce the chances of wrong-side surgery. This was especially important when patients sustained multiple injuries in an explosion, as different injuries might require surgery on different occasions and errors could be caused by that. The ankle patient was an excellent example of that, as he also had an injured right hand and shrapnel in his left thigh. I was not intending to deal with either of those other issues on this occasion and was focussed solely on the ankle. I declared I would not start operating until the patient was marked, so a young surgeon was asked to mark the patient and did so. In addition, the hospital records of the patient were nowhere to be seen in the operating theatre, as the ward had sent the patient for their operation without the notes being available. I insisted the notes should be present before we started, so that my decision could be double-checked. Another young surgeon was sent to retrieve them and did so, in addition to the consent form which had not been signed.

"How do we know this patient agrees with what we are doing?" I asked.

"Of course he does," said an unmasked, unhatted nurse who was scurrying about and helping. "We have his verbal consent."

"Not good enough," I declared. "We must see something in writing and signed by him, or someone on his behalf. While you are at it, please put on a hat and mask."

The nurse shrugged but immediately understood, found a spare consent form in a drawer nearby and the patient signed their consent. The nurse also quickly donned a hat and mask. I was then happy, the patient was certainly happy, and even the nurse understood my approach. It was easy in war for mistakes to be made, such was the immense load of activity. As a population came under increasing pressure, so standards could slip, when in practice that should never happen. The standard of treatment a patient might expect in Gaza should be the same as they might expect in more peaceful surroundings. The type of treatment may be different, but the standard should be identical.

Back in the UK, each of these issues was a major drama and would not normally be allowed to occur. At Al Aqsa in a time of war, the rules had changed. It was why war surgery was so different and why not everyone could do it.

In war surgery, infection was a constant risk and had to be taken seriously, as most of the wounds seen were contaminated. When a building collapsed and a human body was crushed under it, it was more than likely the wounds created would be dirty. Because of this, a war surgeon would generally not stitch a wound closed on the day it happened but would clean the wound first and leave it open. This was called *debridement*. The patient's wound would then be inspected regularly, perhaps debrided further, and only when it looked clean would the wound be stitched closed, or perhaps a skin graft used to cover a large area of raw flesh. Infection was a problem, as it required repeated operations, and might end up with a poor result, longer stay, and probable future disability.

A war surgeon should think infection from the moment they first see a patient and keep thinking infection until it is time for the patient to be discharged. The infection rate at Al Aqsa Hospital was 100 per cent. Every wound was infected – a feature of circumstance.

Part of the problem with infection was how staff behaved in the operating theatre itself, the so-called *aseptic technique*. This was a system of behaviour that was common to operating theatres around the world and that formed part of the basic training for all healthcare staff, irrespective of their role. For most in healthcare, aseptic technique was a reflex that just happened once the principles had been drilled home. Aseptic technique for an orthopaedic surgeon was nearly as critical as food, water, even air. For example, an orthopaedic surgeon would often not have a beard, as that could harbour bacteria, and the surgeon would always wear a facemask in an operating theatre, may well wear an operating hood instead of a hat, and would never walk between a surgeon performing an operation and the instrument trolley nearby. If a surgeon was wearing a sterile operating gown and wished to pass another surgeon dressed the same, the two would turn back-to-back as they passed. These acts were instinctive but essential for keeping infection at bay.

There were many other aspects to aseptic technique, but when the technique failed, so the rates of infection could climb. At Al Aqsa, likely thanks to its huge workload and lack of equipment, medicines, and so much more, aseptic technique was often lacking. I sensed this contributed significantly to the rates of postoperative infection. What was more, whenever I highlighted a shortcoming in aseptic technique, and I had to do so diplomatically, the person whom I was correcting knew precisely what I meant. They may have been offended, I tried hard to avoid that, but they immediately corrected their behaviour and perfect aseptic technique returned. It was as if standards had been allowed to slip, simply because of circumstance, as immediately around the corner lay perfection.

Before darkness fell, I headed back to Rafah once more, along the coastal road. I had decided I should see as much of Gaza as possible while I was there and gather a fuller impression of the tragedy unfolding before me. I saw that as essential. It would also give more space for my colleagues who would be staying at the hospital and not emerge until it was time to go home. It also spared them my snoring.

As I drove south back to Rafah, my mind was filled with questions, as well as plenty of horror. This war was not going away. I was watching what I could only describe as a racial war, an attempt by one side to unpick the civilisation of another. Each hour in Gaza, 15 people were killed, 35 injured, 42 bombs fell, and 12 buildings were destroyed. Meanwhile, the number of tents for IDPs was steadily increasing. All attempts at peace negotiations had so far failed with the conflict now into a win-or-lose situation. It was not a good place to be.

\* \* \*

# Chapter 8

# A Stoical Civilisation

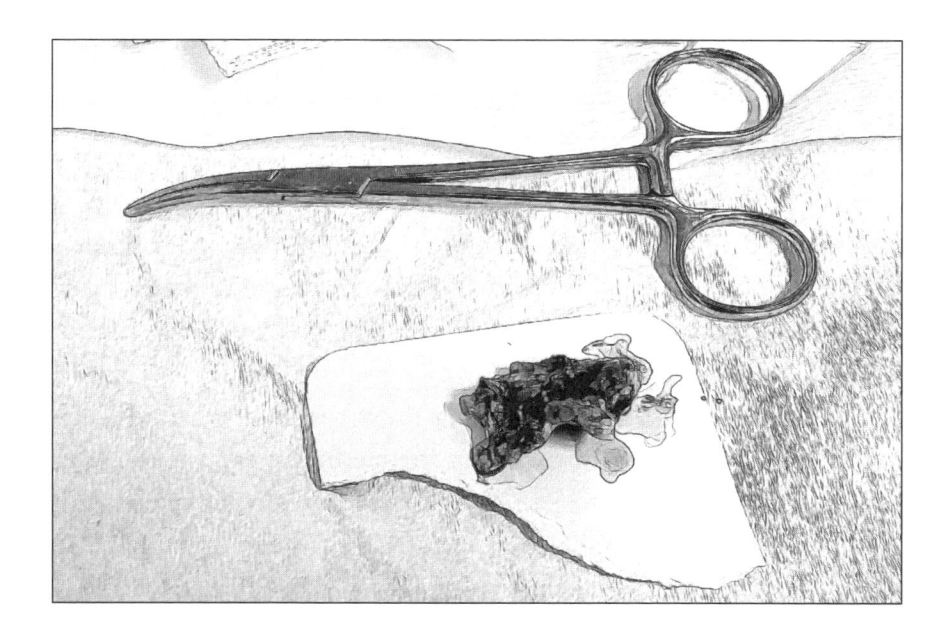

I lay awake for much of the night worrying about the effects on others of what I was doing. The feature of the Gaza war was that it placed me on a permanent adrenaline high. I could not relax for a moment. I had made peace with my Maker that if I never made it home, that was the way it was. In my London flat stood a pile of documentation, ready for retrieval by others should I become incapacitated while in Gaza, whatever the reason. War surgery is a self-centred world and, in many ways, needs to be. Yet back home there were plenty of people who knew I was in Gaza, even if I had told most that I was walking in the French Alps. None of them believed that for a moment.

In Gaza I was surrounded by so much misery, families decimated, children killed for no reason, entire populations displaced with no apparent way out, complete healthcare inadequacy, they were my sole focus. I ignored what was happening back home. Yet it was clear I should not have done so. My patients in the UK with PTSD were clearly suffering thanks to my absence and colleagues had stepped into the breach to help resolve what I had set off. I should have thought, but had not done so, as I was so immersed in the selfishness of war surgery. Next time, should there be one, I must be different.

My family, too. My wife, children, grandchildren, sister, and so many in addition. Some were praying, some hoping, some listening to each news bulletin throughout the day and night. Whenever a tragedy occurred, and Gaza was constant unhappiness, to those back home I was the one involved. At the medical frontline as I was, I might easily have been unaffected, even unaware, or geographically separate, but not to those I had left behind. To them, each tragedy affected me, and by proxy affected them. In some respects, those back home had a harder time than those like me at the tip of the medical spear. I must never forget this, which was why I had lain awake most of the night worrying.

Back at Al Aqsa Hospital, after a further drive along the coast to reach it and watched for my entire journey by an overhead *zinnanah*, I was rapidly immersed into the emotion of the tragedy that was Gaza. I was stopped by a Palestinian woman in the middle of my ward round. She was aged in her late sixties, knew I was from the UK, and she wished to speak. This is what she said:

> *"My house down, I haven't my children, every member of my family died, 26 persons died. I haven't house, I haven't my family, I haven't children, I haven't food, I have lost everything, I haven't money. I don't know what I can do. All Palestinians like me. What can we do? Please you ask for all Europe listen to me please."*

The woman's English was not the best but was certainly better than my Arabic. Her message was clear. She represented just one person of many and described an individual, almost insurmountable tragedy.

Yet her English was sufficiently good to pass her message, which she did successfully. I found it difficult to continue work that day after I had heard her words, but when it came to the care of the victims of war the only choice I had was to keep going. It was my only option and was not a time to turn and run.

There were so many patients milling through Al Aqsa Hospital, there was almost no need to seek out work. Had I managed to find a small table and set it down in a corner, within moments I would have been surrounded by Palestinians seeking advice. As it was, all I needed do was stand and let the work come to me.

"Please doctor, look at this," said a mother, as she produced her mobile telephone and showed me the X-ray images of her 8-year-old child, somewhere in an outside tent, and the child's two broken thighbones.

"No, doctor, do not look at that. Look at this," would say another, again a mother as she tried to interrupt. Out would come the obligatory mobile and this time I would be shown the X-ray of another child, who was on a mattress in an external stairwell of the hospital's administration block. The child had been hiding from missiles in a nearby camp but the sheltering had been worthless. The result had been an amputated forearm, a crushed chest, and a broken shin bone, in addition to an open shin wound that was contaminated. "Please help us," appealed the mother.

Or the brother of a middle-aged woman, a woman who had been widowed by shellfire. The brother had brought images of the widow's right leg, which had been amputated mid-thigh by the explosion. Somehow she had not bled to death. The pictures were not well taken but were sufficient to explain the tragedy.

These patients were each shown to me within a ten-minute period that morning. There was plenty to do at Al Aqsa Hospital and no way anyone might keep pace. The workload was far beyond anything that was manageable.

A common request from the injured was to seek the removal of shrapnel. There was plenty of shrapnel to see as so many of the injuries were because of explosive devices. Generally, I would leave shrapnel alone, as to find it ran the risk of causing problems. Often the shrapnel could lie next to a bone, or beside a vital nerve or blood vessel, so it was possible to do more damage by retrieving the shrapnel than to leave it where it is was. However, occasionally shrapnel had to be removed, or a casualty could not be persuaded that leaving it alone was safer than trying to find it surgically. Commonly, the hole created by the shrapnel's entry was a long way from the shrapnel itself. A patient might thus require a very large incision and a long period in the operating theatre to find what might turn out to be a small fragment of metal. Large incisions and long operations should be avoided during war as both are a recipe for wound infection. At Al Aqsa Hospital, shrapnel removal was also not regarded as an emergency, so the procedure would often be performed in one of the three temporary operating theatres that had once been maternity delivery suites. The suites were not surgically clean and did not carry critical items of equipment such as decent lighting or cautery, which were often needed if a blood vessel was cut unexpectedly. Yet for one particular patient I did agree to remove some shrapnel, as he had a wound on the back of his left thigh that was failing to heal, the shrapnel beneath the wound preventing that from happening.

To be sure I could find the shrapnel, I kept an X-ray machine alongside me during surgery. I made no incision at all until I had used a metal probe on the patient's skin to identify the location of the shrapnel deep within by using the X-ray machine. Once I was satisfied that I had located the shrapnel, I made as small an incision as I could, inserted my gloved little finger into the wound, felt for and identified the location of the shrapnel, inserted a surgical grabber, and out the shrapnel came. This allowed me to limit the size of the surgical wound needed as well as reducing the length of time the procedure took. I considered this to be the best way of minimising the risk of infection occurring after surgery. My caution paid off, as the wound healed speedily, and the patient was delighted. He never knew how much I had worried before performing what to him was a small procedure but to me was huge. The shrapnel turned out to be larger than I had thought.

Families, at least the survivors, were extremely important at Al Aqsa, as there were so few nurses to undertake routine tasks on the wards. War casualties would thus bring into the hospital as many members of their family as they could, and even take over a portion of ward so they could all be together. Hospitals were seen as safer places than anywhere outside, even though it seemed to be open house on healthcare facilities in the free-fire zone called Gaza. All one could say was there was less free fire in a hospital than might be experienced beyond its walls. It was the risk I ran twice daily when driving to and from Rafah. The family would change dressings, clean the floor around the patient, provide physiotherapy, wash the patient, change any bedding, and cook their food. Patients would frequently be unable to walk, and there were insufficient wheelchairs available to allow a patient to be taken to a toilet. Many patients were thus placed in nappies so that a bedpan had neither to be used nor emptied. Without the family to support a patient, healthcare at Al Aqsa would have been impossible. There were simply insufficient staff members to do the job. It did not matter if no member of the family had any medical training. To watch families pull together, despite the terrible circumstances, was impressive.

With rates of infection so high it was important not to accept that as normal, but to do everything possible to reduce the rate where feasible. Improvement in aseptic technique both generally and in the operating theatre was one way but reducing the frequency of changing a dressing was another. Because wounds were so often contaminated, the wound needed to be cleaned many times before it could be stitched closed or covered with a skin graft. Each cleaning, certainly in the operating theatre, required a general anaesthetic as well. However, it had become routine practice at Al Aqsa to change every dressing daily, which meant many dressings would be done each day in the operating theatre complex. Commonly, there would be 30-40 dressing changes every day, in addition to any surgery that might be required. As well as the dressing changes in the operating theatres, there were also smaller dressing changes needed elsewhere, either in tents located in the hospital courtyard by MSF, or directly on the ward by families and occasional volunteer nurses. Each change of dressing was a risk of infection.

Compare that with what has become routine practice in more peaceful parts of the world. Dressings are only changed if they become soiled and open wounds are inspected only every 2-3 days. I tried to institute this at Al Aqsa Hospital but I failed. However, to reduce the number of dressing changes from daily to every other day would instantly halve the number of dressings needed, and free up badly needed operating space. To me it was a simple solution, but I do not think I succeeded in persuading others to try. It was a battle that I one day hope to win.

A problem with there being so much trauma was that routine conditions that might have been given priority under normal circumstances soon became forgotten. The cancer of the lung that needed radiotherapy, or perhaps the cancer of the prostate that required chemotherapy. These were unfortunate conditions that were commonly seen throughout the world and in less frenetic circumstances would be treated appropriately. In Gaza the situation was different. Routine conditions were often side-lined and quite possibly forgotten. Their management relied on family members pushing, shoving, scraping, and begging so that a relative was kept in focus and a medic's attention was not diverted towards other more pressing needs. Without family support once again, patients with routine conditions could be forgotten and all the while a tumour would expand. There was a list of patients for evacuation beyond Gaza's frontiers, to places such as Egypt and Jordan. Patients on the list did not know where they might be headed, nor when, nor for how long and required Israel's permission before they could be evacuated anyway. Many of the patients were victims of war but plenty were those with forgotten conditions. The list carried nearly 10,000 names, and was steadily lengthening. There was no chance they would all be evacuated.

Despite warfare chaos all around, the Palestinian population was trying to maintain as much normality as it could. That included going to the barber, just as I had done in London before heading for Gaza. Until I reached the territory, I felt sure my hair was the perfect length but when I saw what the locals regarded as a proper haircut, I could understand why they thought mine was long. Perhaps, I reflected, it was time to try a Palestinian haircut. After all, I now had the Arab name of Abu Ruairidh, why not a haircut, too? The two hospital barbers were very busy and worked both indoors and out. When outside they were directly under the flight path of the *zinnanah*. Occasionally I saw one of the barbers wave his cut-throat razor fiercely at the *zinnanah*, although whether his manifestly aggressive message made it back to IDF headquarters, I will never know.

At one point, when one of the barbers was hard at work with a patient, who was sadly also a triple amputee thanks to an Israeli missile, I stopped to see more closely what they were doing. My interest was all that it took.

"Doctor, doctor!" exclaimed the barbers. "Let me cut your hair. I will do it for free!"

Radical would be an understatement for what the triple amputee was undergoing, although he seemed totally happy with the result. Yet it was far too short for my liking and, what was more, was being perfomed with a cut-throat razor. However much I had been learning to trust the locals, I was unsure that trust would extend to allowing a cut-throat to be used near my gullet. Security would have gone crazy and once again I would have been in trouble. I left my hair alone.

Generally, the Palestinians impressed me as a nation, as they had been through so much, with plenty more ahead, and I never once heard a Palestinian make a fuss. I could not say the same for other nationalities, who would fuss continually, but being stoical was clearly the Palestinian way. One 60-year-old man I met exemplified this perfectly. He had unexpectedly rounded a corner four months earlier and came face-to-face with an Israeli tank. He was unarmed, as were all the Palestinians I ever met in Gaza. I never once saw a weapon anywhere in the territory. The man played chicken with the tank, but the tank did not play chicken with him and opened fire. The Israeli tank mostly missed but not completely, and the man had time to duck behind cover. The tank did not follow. The Palestinian was left with part of his left upper arm bone destroyed, part missing, and two nerves damaged. He came to seek my advice. Sadly, although his once open wounds had by then healed, I could not think of an operation that would help but certainly rehabilitation would do something. There was no physiotherapy of note in the hospital and, anyway, the man lived outside in an IDP tented camp. So together we fashioned an exercise regime for his shoulder with me showing him what was needed and the Palestinian following suit. Fifteen minutes later we were done, and the Palestinian had his exercise regime. As for his playing chicken with a tank, that was impressive. The man was seriously hard core and an excellent example of why the Palestinian nation impressed me. He never complained once.

Overall, the war had been reasonably quiet for the past day, and I had not heard any shells or missiles, although had to strain hard to listen as I was now becoming accustomed to crumps, thumps, and rat-ta-tat-tats around me. Several F16 fighter jets had flown overhead but they did not appear interested in us and were off to make their mischief somewhere different. Yet judging by the lower rate of distant explosions the battles appeared less ferocious. I did not wish to be optimistic, but realised ceasefire talks were at fever pitch in Cairo and that Hamas had sent a negotiating group to the city, which was a vaguely positive sign. Hamas was demanding a permanent ceasefire, the withdrawal of the Israeli army from Gaza and the return of displaced people to their homes, in addition to other items as well. There had also been some cross-border fire between Israel and Lebanon while Jordan stated publicly that an invasion of Rafah should not be allowed. I was pleased to hear that as I was spending every night in Rafah and had no desire for that to change. When I drove through the streets of

Rafah, I could not see how the Israelis could possibly invade the city without creating many innocent casualties. The density of displaced people was huge, and they truly had nowhere to go. A tent offers zero protection from a missile. Hamas had also announced that it had killed 14 Israeli soldiers around Khan Yunis, which matched with the Israeli refusal of our request to visit the city in case we needed to move from Al Aqsa Hospital. It made sense to have a Plan B. So far, we only had a Plan A, but we had yet to make it to Khan Yunis.

\* \* \*

That tiny speck on the horizon is a warship waiting, looking and…

The mushroom cloud from an exploding missile in the distance.

IDP camp with litter all around.

Overflowing sewage right beside a water collection point and an IDP camp – what chance is there to stay healthy?

Entrance to Al Aqsa Hospital in Deir-al-Balah.

The hospital was very overcrowded.

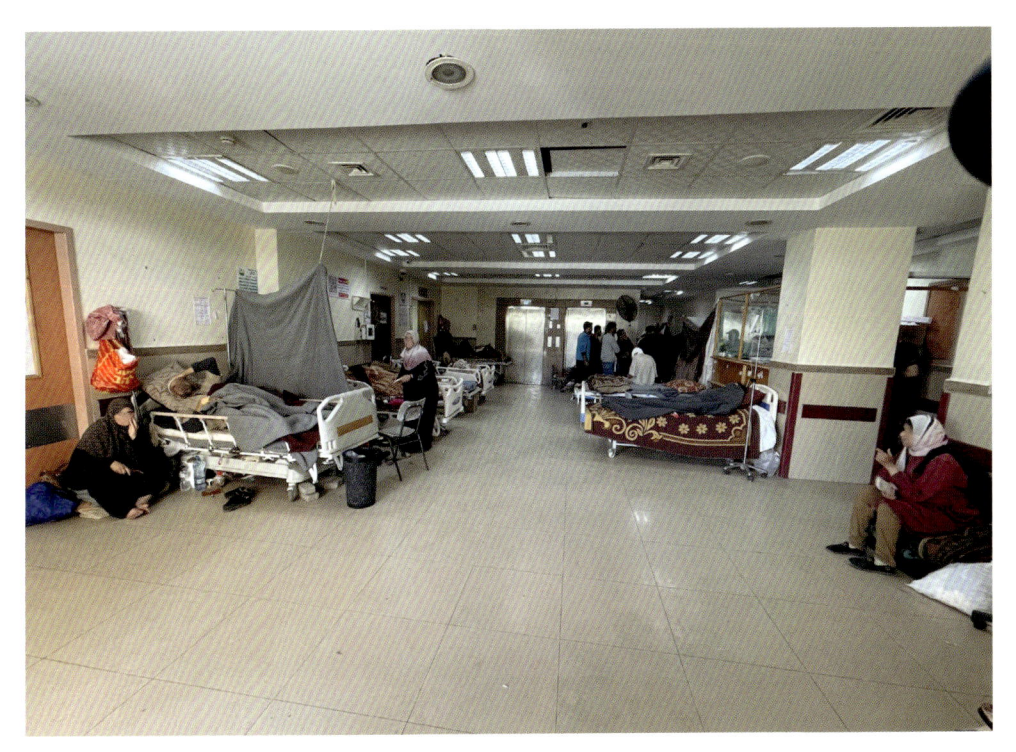

Hospital reception had become a ward.

Corridors became wards with patients staying for lengthy periods.

Space being constructed for at least another 100 patients, likely even more.

The hospital's storeroom contained items that nobody knew were there.

Fragmentation film on the hospital's windows which are kept slightly ajar – in case of an explosion.

Many Gazans set up camp in the hospital's grounds on the basis it might be safer.

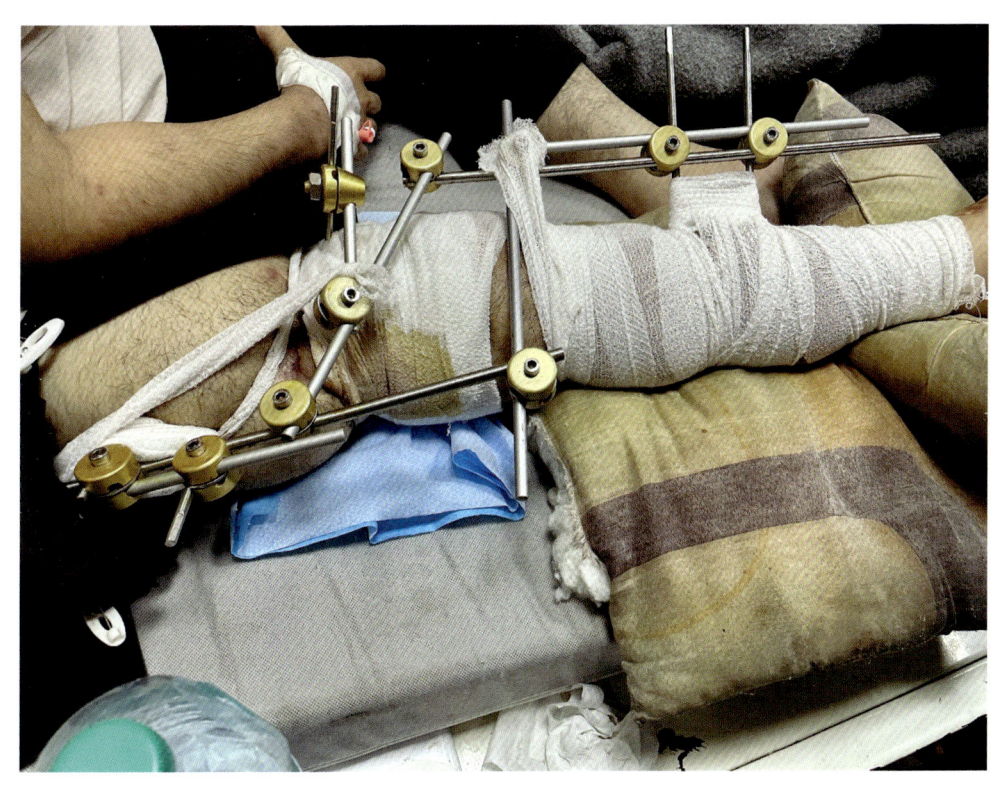

An external fixator in position – plenty of these were needed.

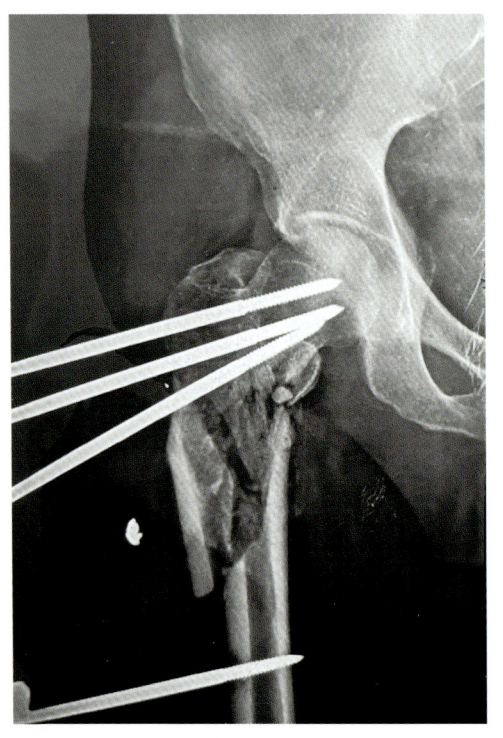

Broken thighbone and shrapnel in a surgeon.

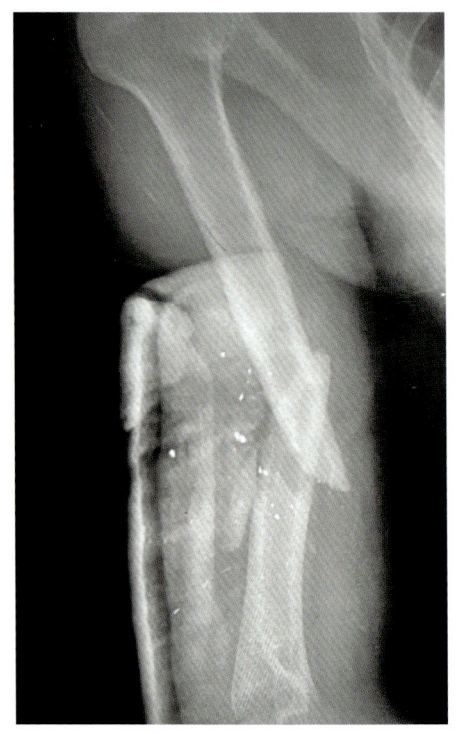

Shrapnel from an explosion has broken this arm bone (humerus).

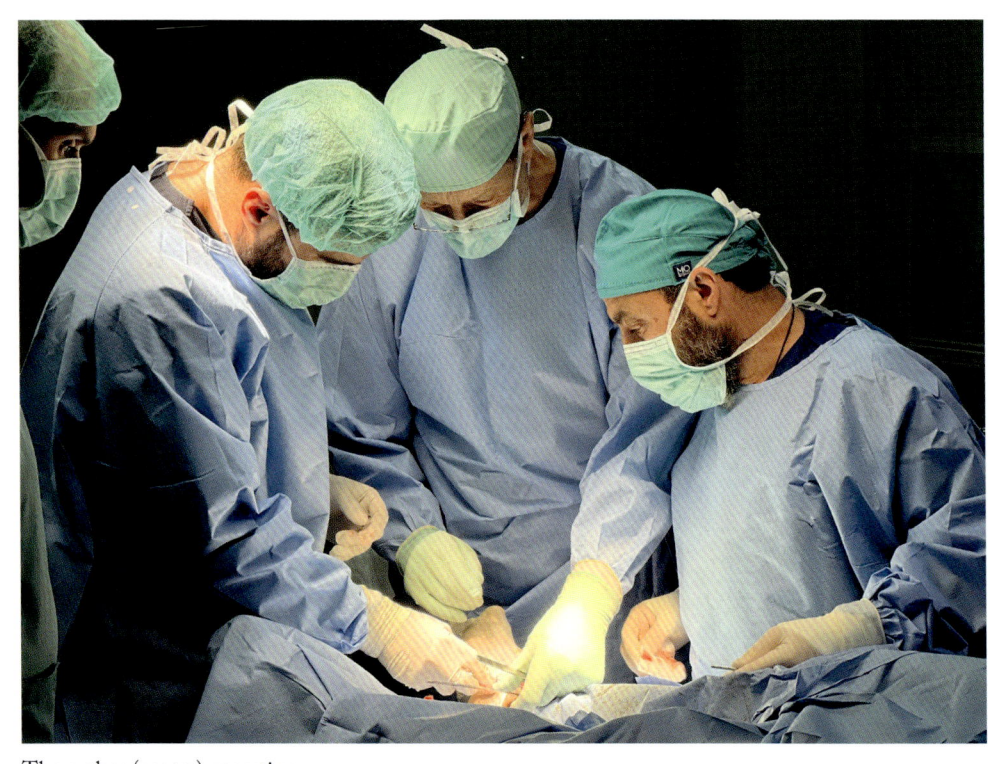

The author (centre) operating.

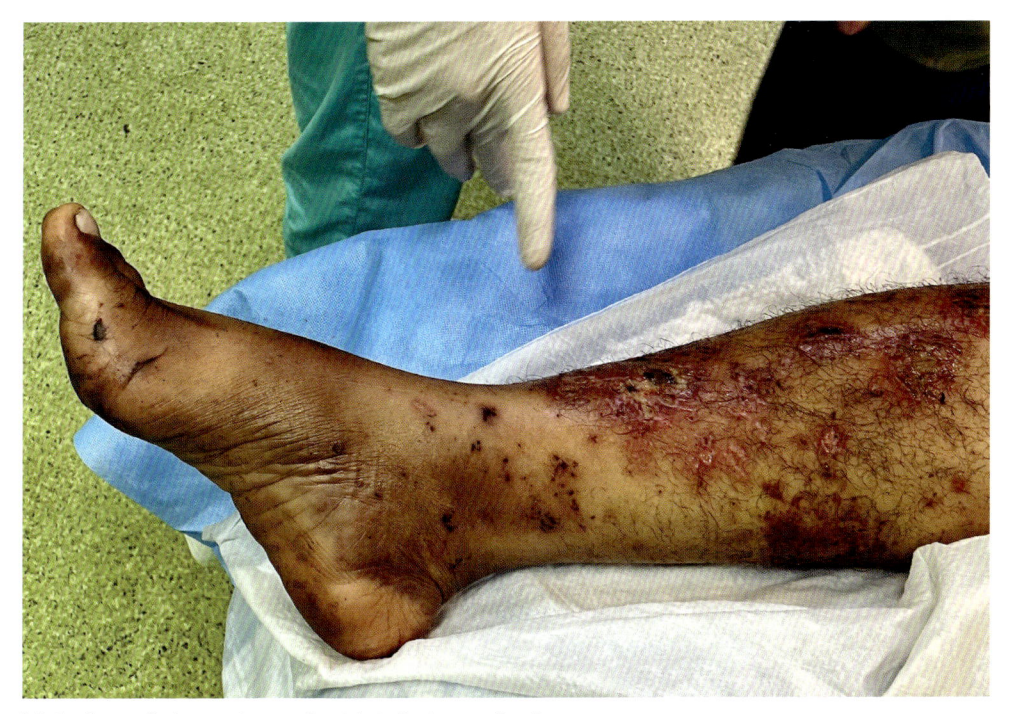

Multiple small shrapnel wounds with infection setting in.

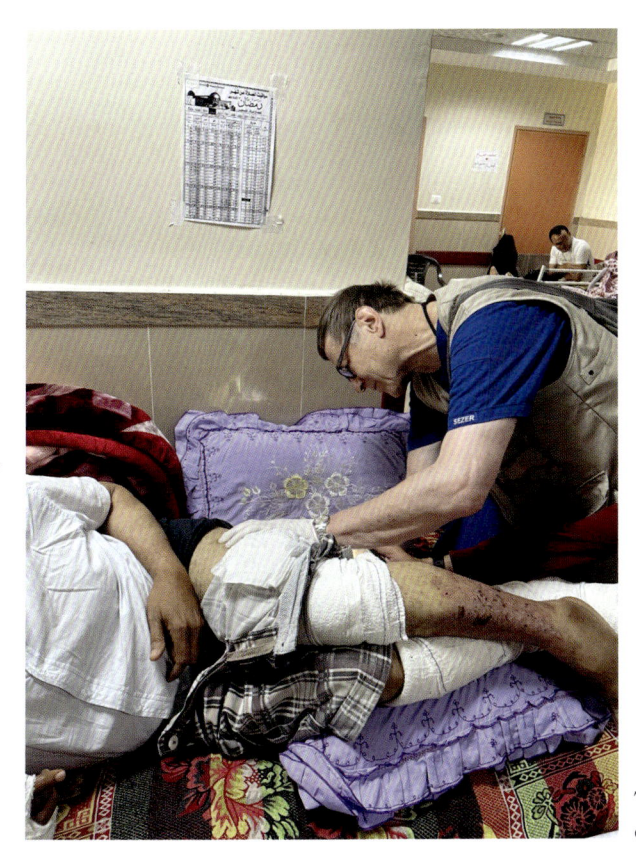

The author on a ward round examining a patient's thigh.

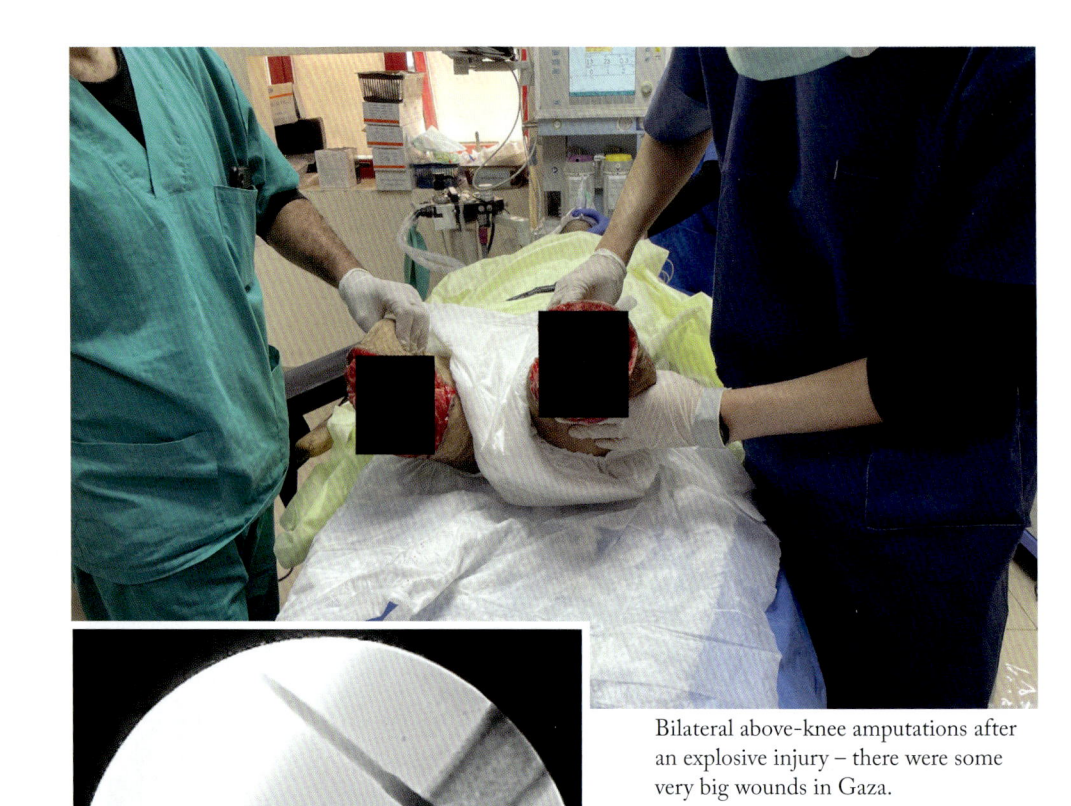

Bilateral above-knee amputations after an explosive injury – there were some very big wounds in Gaza.

Straight metal marker placed on the skin to identify the location of an irregular piece of shrapnel before an incision is made. The shrapnel is very close to the bone.

The shrapnel was larger than I had thought.

# Chapter 9

# War is About People

Food in Gaza was in short supply, and I was already down to a single meal per day. So far it had been rice and something, with the something mostly being chicken, but darker on occasion. I guessed the darker meat was lamb but did not know and thought it safer not to ask. They did not say, I did not inquire, while the meal was just what I needed. Perhaps one day I will be told what I had eaten. Whatever its origin, it was tasty.

I had brought food from London just in case and had not realised that one meal each day was all I would be receiving. I should have guessed. The food I had brought was partly in case of so-called *hibernation*, which is when the going becomes bad in a war zone and humanitarian workers must go to ground, hide, and wait for threats to diminish. I had seen several bags already positioned and in place, marked as being food for hibernation, so felt it would be safe to open my own food to cover my breakfast, which I did. I am glad I did so. I had pondered extensively in the UK what I should bring, had dallied near many supermarket shelves, but had finally chosen to take my favourite, ready-to-eat meals packed for the mountains. I sometimes eat them when I am out and about on the UK's fells. It was why, when I awoke in Rafah to the sound of an overhead *zinnanah*, a cockerel crowing, house sparrows tweeting, and a *muazzim* summoning, my first act was to reach from my bed, grab my meal and tuck right into meatballs and pasta. Second only to ready-to-eat chocolate pudding, and I had some of that in my rations as well, meatballs and pasta were my favourite. I slobbered, munched, and crunched noisily and had consumed the packet within moments.

Because of the high inflation rate in Gaza, simple food items, if available at all, had become hard to obtain and were frequently very expensive. For example, at one point, a single chicken's egg cost US$8 – a fortune anywhere, but especially in Gaza. This turned many Palestinians into criminals, so not all injuries I saw at Al Aqsa were the result of warfare. One patient had both shin bones broken by the local police, who beat him for stealing from bombed houses.

Food was a big issue in Gaza, as a famine was developing that was the first example of an entirely man-made famine this century. Famines were established events elsewhere as well, for example in South Sudan and Somalia, but the causes there included conflict in addition to economic and environmental shocks. Gaza was different and I could see that with my patients. It was rare to see people eating, whether in the hospital or outside. The lack of food made people more likely to develop infectious diseases, poor oral health, injury, depression and anxiety disorders, heart disease, hypertension, arthritis, and plenty more. With so much infection around in the hospital anyway, patients needed as much resistance as possible, but with lack of food, their ability to resist and fight infection was limited.

To make this slightly more scientific, there is something called the Integrated Food Security Phase Classification (IPC) that was developed in 2004 to classify the characteristics of the food and nutrition crisis in Somalia at that time. This classification is used globally today to assess crises. It is a five-phase scale, as follows:

IPC1 – minimal; IPC2 – stressed; IPC3 – crisis;
IPC4 – emergency; IPC5 – famine.

To be declared IPC5 (famine), three criteria must be met. At least 20 per cent of households should face acute food insecurity or an extreme lack of food, 30 per cent of children should suffer from acute malnutrition, and two adults (or four children) must die daily from either starvation or the interaction of malnutrition and disease. It is this final category that is important for a war surgeon as it can dramatically influence the outcomes of surgery.

In Gaza, by mid-March 2024 the entire population had been classified as being IPC3, 4 or 5. Those in the north were likely to be IPC5 while those in the south were slightly better off. There were no examples of IPC1 or 2 in the territory. Most households had been missing meals daily and some had been going entire days and nights without eating. This occurred in 80 per cent of households in the north and among some of the IDPs in the south. Lack of food in Gaza was a drama, so I could hardly object to my one meal each day when most locals had nothing.

Perhaps more remarkable was the fact that it was Ramadan, that time of Muslim fasting. Despite famine being on the rise, the observation of Ramadan was widespread. Remarkable. As a Christian I was trying hard to join in. There are few periods of observance that emphasise religious differences better than Ramadan. Yet I would sometimes fail and had to sneak a slurp of bottled water in a loo or cupboard when I hoped no one was looking. The locals were more than understanding if I was ever caught. Ramadan is also a period of extreme kindness.

Even with warfare around, and the dead and injured being brought to the hospital, it was astonishing how the Palestinians still had time for fasting. I wondered how many other nations might have achieved this. I doubted many would.

Ramadan generally allows two meals daily. There is the pre-dawn *suhoor* and the post-dawn *iftar*. There are some who prefer not to get up early for the pre-dawn *suhoor* and thus focus solely on one meal each day, the *iftar*. That is even more remarkable.

My optimism that something positive would come out of the peace talks in Cairo was wavering, as there were still *zinnanah* buzzing above me and no evidence of anything changing on the ground, whatever the global news bulletins claimed. Whether the *zinnanah* were just watching, or about to target some poor soul, adding to the undoubted massive collateral damage to property and innocent victims, was anyone's guess. I will never hear the buzz of a model airplane on my local UK common in the same way again. It sounds just like a *zinnanah*. That will be me straight under the nearest table, not that tables are any good against missiles.

There were rumblings in the press that Israel was planning a major troop withdrawal from southern Gaza imminently. You could have fooled me. In addition to the *zinnanah*, there were some large explosions last night around Khan Yunis, 9.59 kilometres (5.96 miles) from Rafah, when some houses were reduced to rubble. There was still plenty of fighting in progress, easily audible from Rafah.

If there was any doubt about ongoing fighting, a 16-year-old boy arrived as an emergency in the morning and was admitted directly to Al Aqsa Hospital's Resuscitation Room, which lay just to one side of the Emergency Department. The boy reached the hospital within 30 minutes of being wounded in his left thigh by what looked to be multiple pieces of shrapnel from an explosion. I never did establish what he was doing when injured. There were at least seven individual holes in the thigh, each one bleeding, but the shrapnel, we subsequently established but did not know on his arrival, had somehow missed everything vital. His major blood vessels and thighbone were intact. I have no clue how they were not damaged, but an invisible hand was helping the boy that morning.

When we first saw the boy, we had no way of knowing if major structures had been damaged, so assumed the worst. It is the only way with emergencies. A tourniquet was placed around his upper thigh to control the bleeding as he had lost so much blood. His blood pressure was falling and his pulse rate rising, a situation that medics call *haemorrhagic shock*, so it was important to control the blood loss. Fourteen members of healthcare staff worked on the casualty, who was soon in the operating theatre and being treated. It was a remarkable demonstration of what can be achieved in a war zone, and that it is truly important to reach medical care speedily so that a casualty can receive the best treatment available. The boy was also a reminder of how important it was to control bleeding. In battle, more than 90 per cent of those who die perish simply because they bleed to death, the so-called *bleeding out*. The training we had received in Cairo on how to apply a tourniquet made instant sense, as the tourniquet around the boy's thigh helped save his life. It allowed the medics to work on him before sending him to the operating theatre, where emergency surgery brought the situation under control. However, the boy also showed that whatever the news bulletins might have been saying about peace talks, the ground war continued. There was no escaping it.

With the ever-increasing demand for operating theatre space, and as the casualty load continued, all operations needed to be booked, an anaesthetist found, nurses sought, rooms cleaned, radiographers hunted, limited instruments got ready, and plenty more besides. One case might be a wounded leg, the next a fractured skull, the next a broken arm, then an abdomen, then some shrapnel in the heart, and so on. The range of injuries seen at Al Aqsa was astonishing. You name it and the injury would have featured sometime, but one never knew what might come through the door. There is little purpose in being too specialist with war surgery as a surgeon must do just about anything. There is no room for claiming ignorance when a human life is at stake. You do the best you can with what you have, and that is it.

However, to gain access to an operating theatre cannot be taken for granted even when war is being waged all around. Each case must be negotiated with the senior nurse in charge of the operating theatre complex and I was useless at it. I would hide behind my local colleagues when negotiation was underway and listen to them humbly as they struck some deal to allow a patient into the operating theatre. The default position of the senior nurse was that a case could not be done and that another victim of warfare took priority. My job, at least those bargaining on my behalf, was to persuade the senior nurse that my case was more important.

The conversation, which would be held standing in the busy operating theatre corridor with patients left, right and everywhere, would run something like this:

*Senior nurse*: "Your patient does not sound too bad. You can do him later in one of the delivery suites."

*Me* (actually a local on my behalf): "She's dying. Actively bleeding. I must get into theatre quickly."

*Senior nurse*: "Give her some blood. She'll wait."

*Me*: "We haven't got any."

*Senior nurse*: "Plasma expander then."

*Me*: "We haven't got any of that either."

*Senior nurse*: "The theatres are full. Booked up for the next five hours. You'll have to wait."

*Me*: "She'll be dead by then."

*Senior nurse*: "OK, but you'll have to be quick. Can you get it done in no more than 30 minutes?"

*Me*: "No problems."

*Senior nurse*: "That's fine then. Theatre 1, the emergency operating theatre, is yours for 30 minutes, starting in 10 minutes' time. Don't be late or slow. There is a pile of casualties waiting."

With that, I was in, having promised to finish the case in double-quick time, although I doubted anything I pledged was possible. In the event, it would take me two hours to finish the case, not the 30 minutes I had promised, but it was all part of the bargaining process. It was simply the way things were done at Al Aqsa Hospital.

Negotiating theatre space was important as the senior nurse had to show who was boss. That was certainly not me. Once the theatre slot had been agreed, the patient was brought to the theatre suite by their family or friends. There was no portering service remaining at Al Aqsa Hospital, it had long since been dismantled or destroyed.

Negotiating space in an operating theatre was a good example of aspects of war surgery that many do not see. Warfare as a medic is not just about operating and saving lives. In fact, that is only a small part of a medic's activity. I would estimate that an operation is at best 25 per cent of the total care of a casualty. However well an operation may be performed, it is of no use unless the patient has been adequately prepared beforehand, the investigations are adequate, and the postoperative care and rehabilitation thought through.

Much of what is necessary is to maintain personal contact, talk and smile copiously, and meet people as much as one can rather than relying on emails and text messages. Warfare is an unnatural environment and everyone, bar none, is on edge even if they do not feel that. An outsider can see it, even if the individual says they are relaxed and well. In war zones, I make sure that I spend considerable chunks of time talking to others and would much prefer to see someone in the flesh, sit down, smile, talk about many things in addition to the reason I wished to speak with them in the first place. It is very easy for those at the frontline to ignore emotions, not just their own but those of others, too. It is well worth taking time to chat even if theoretically all a request needs is a telephone call, text, or social media message.

In any event, I am always suspicious of messages I both send and receive. There have been too many instances where messages have been delayed, gone missing, or have appeared corrupted. On one occasion even my laptop keyboard ceased to work but miraculously recovered the moment I crossed the Gaza frontier into an adjacent land. I have long worked on the basis that everything I do electronically, in whatever form, is seen by a mysterious Face somewhere on the planet. The Face will know what I am doing even before I know it myself and will certainly know where I am located. It is why I forge a clear medical path when in zones of conflict as I do not want The Face to see me as being anything other than medical. Secretly, this is a blessing, as it means I am forced to see someone directly and not rely on my mobile or laptop, which in a war zone are the same as sending a postcard home. I have no idea if The Face is Abraham, Mohammed, or someone completely different but it makes sense to assume everything electronic is insecure.

There will be human agents as well, gathering what the spooks call HUMINT. They will be impossible to spot, so do not even try. Stick to what you know and make it clear throughout that you are medical. In warfare, that is your protection and is precisely how I behave. Talk and chat as much as you can. Use electronics as little as possible, ideally not at all.

It is important to remain apolitical in warfare, and not be seen to support any side. Stick to what you know and are good at. It is likely that taking a stance back home is why you have gone to a war zone at all, but when at the tip of the medical spear, stay neutral, however strong your emotion. Out there and having a go at both each other and collateral civilians, are plenty of locals who are passionate but there are many outsiders as well. Israel has a long history of using mercenaries for its fighting. A weekly payment of US$4,300 may be part of the reason. The French radio network Europe1 at one time revealed that there were 4,185 French/Israeli dual citizens who had joined the Israeli army for the Gaza conflict. France is but one of many nations that has supplied fighters for the war. For reasons that escape me, such individuals are portrayed as heroes in the Gaza war but would be seen as war criminals somewhere else. I will leave that distinction to politicians.

Not a single European country, nor the US, and nor the UK, has publicly warned their own citizens against joining the IDF. Meanwhile South Africa has warned individuals who enlist in the Israeli army that they risk losing their citizenship. It is more than likely that foreign fighters – mercenaries – have been involved in many of the killings that have taken place during this Gaza conflict. Your job as a medic is to stay neutral. Never forget that, even if your own nationals are complicit in what may elsewhere be regarded as war crimes. War surgery is a strange specialty, but you are no use to your patients dead. Do everything to stay in one piece.

Sometime before dark, and watched by an overhead *zinnanah*, I drove the 90-minute journey back to Rafah along what was once a golden Mediterranean coast. Deir-al-Balah's sewage overflow was becoming worse, and was littered with plastic debris, which seemed to be speedily accumulating in Gaza. On this occasion I had to take a different route because there was so much traffic and it was barely possible to make any progress at all. There was a skill to driving in Gaza, which I did not possess, so am glad I was provided with an official driver. The skill was to completely ignore all other vehicles on the road and to behave utterly selfishly. Meanwhile pedestrians would walk on the road, and certainly cross it, without looking in any direction. You could not afford to hit a pedestrian, as that would have created local mayhem, someone could have produced a weapon, and I would not have made it home.

Kite flying was a popular pastime for children in Gaza, especially during the windier months, which are from October to March. The windiest month is February. Gazans have a long history of kite-making and flying, connected with symbolic calls for freedom among Palestinians during the ongoing war. Gazans even set a Guinness World

Record in 2011 for the most kites flown simultaneously, flying over 12,000 kites in one day. Children used to play football extensively, but there was little space between the tents, so football was less possible. Many of the children thus took to flying kites instead and I could frequently see plenty of them flapping and diving overhead, especially towards the end of the day. Kites were also a means of disobeying the Israeli restrictions on the use of airspace, especially if a kite carried the Palestinian colours of three equal horizontal stripes – black, white, and green from top to bottom. There was thus a degree of protest, too. Sadly, many become accidentally caught in overhead cables, so I became accustomed to seeing many kites flying during my regular drives to Rafah, but many dead ones trapped by overhead cables as well.

Kites are also reminiscent of a well-known Gazan poet, Refaat Alareer, who received many warnings of his imminent death from Israel. He was sadly killed in the end, on 6 December 2023, alongside his brother, sister, and their children. Five weeks before this tragedy he wrote the instantly classic poem *If I must die*, which has now been translated into many languages and goes as follows:

> *If I must die,*
> *you must live*
> *to tell my story*
> *to sell my things*
> *to buy a piece of cloth*
> *and some strings,*
> *(make it white with a long tail)*
> *so that a child, somewhere in Gaza*
> *while looking heaven in the eye*
> *awaiting his dad who left in a blaze –*
> *and bid no one farewell*
> *not even to his flesh*
> *not even to himself –*
> *sees the kite, my kite you made, flying up above*

*and thinks for a moment an angel is there*
*bringing back love*
*If I must die*
*let it bring hope*
*let it be a tale*

If you can read this poem without shedding a tear, you are far stronger than me.

A feature of the increasing poverty and food shortages in Gaza, on my journey to Rafah three children tried to break into the car. They shouted, "Money! Money!" all the while. I pretended not to notice, even if instinctively I wanted to get out of the car and thump them. The children were so committed that they hung on to the car as we drove past slowly. It was impossible to go fast because of the dense traffic, pedestrians, collapsing tents, donkeys, camels, and wobbling cyclists. The threesome banged on the door, furiously worked its handle only to find the door locked, as they attempted to steal the items I had left on the back seat. In the end their antics and efforts became too much, so the driver stopped the car, insisted I stayed seated, clambered out himself, and shouted at the children in Arabic. Within moments they had made their escape, and never looked back. In one respect I was relieved, in another saddened. During normal times the three children would never have behaved in that way.

The dirt-track roads were perhaps fuller than normal, as Israel had announced it would be undertaking a major pull-out from Gaza. However, in case there was any chance of our relaxation and optimism, they also claimed they were pulling out to prepare for further operations. This included an invasion of Rafah. Previously, Israeli withdrawals had been part of a bigger picture, and I saw the same pattern with this most recent pledge. For example, they pulled out of the area around Al Shifa Hospital in Gaza City and then returned to demolish the place. They did the same for Nasser Hospital in Khan Yunis. Consequently, I had my doubts about how long an Israeli withdrawal would last. With approximately 125 Israeli hostages still in Hamas' hands, I could not see Israel withdrawing for long. If I had learned nothing else during the Gaza conflict, it was that everything occurred for a reason and there was no such thing as being kind.

\* \* \*

# Chapter 10

# Huge Wounds and Mental Health

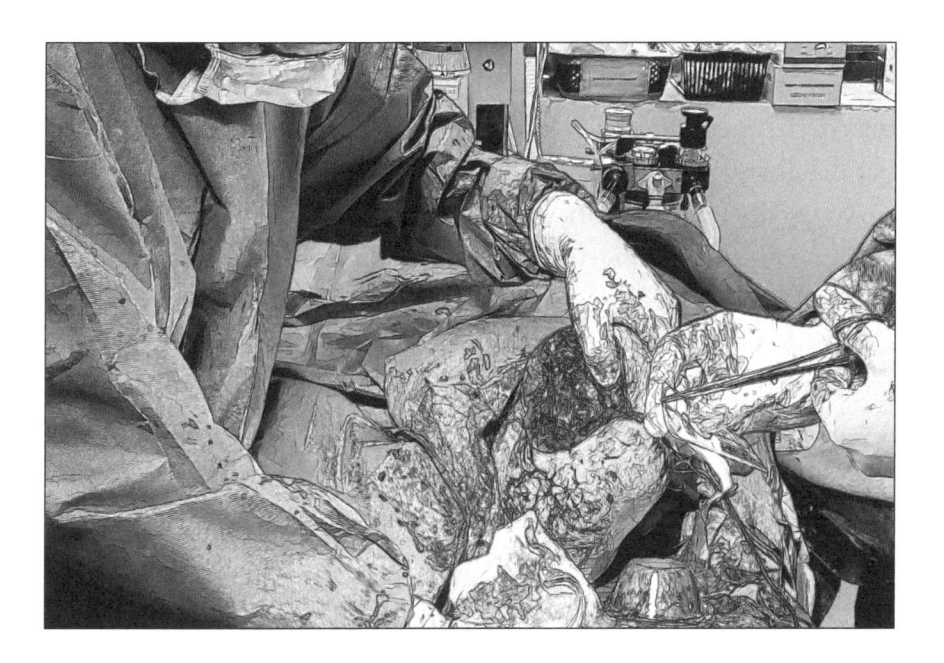

To take both a Geiger counter and air quality meter into Gaza from the UK had not been an easy task. I had wrapped them in multiple layers of spare clothing so as not to attract attention, just about hid the meters from myself and nearly forgot to use them. Almost on the spur of one moment I remembered, and in between operations and ward rounds I used both, to establish how safe the hidden environment was around me. There is a tendency for staff during warfare to ignore their own safety, so concerned are they with the welfare of others. Yet with a conflict that had already been going for six months and was likely to continue for a good deal longer, staff welfare was an issue.

To my surprise, the Geiger counter revealed nothing suspicious, despite conflict all around. A Geiger counter measures in counts per minute, with a low level of background radiation being normal. The average natural background radiation is between 5 and 60 counts per minute (cpm). For Al Aqsa Hospital, in the outdoor hospital courtyard, the background count was 10cpm. This became slightly more than double, at 22cpm, when I measured radiation in both X-ray and CT scan departments, but such levels were still acceptable. I was surprised but delighted to see this.

Air quality was sadly different. Indeed, I was horrified, as it appeared I had no chance of long-term survival, even if the shells and missiles had stopped right away. The acceptable level of Volatile Organic Compounds in the air is <0.3mg/m$^3$ while at Al Aqsa Hospital I measured it at 0.927mg/m$^3$. This level was way over the top, and I am thus destined for eye, nose and throat irritation, upper respiratory tract infections, nausea, allergic reactions, and headaches, in addition to lung cancer and heart disease. The hospital's carbon dioxide ($CO_2$) levels were also way above acceptable, as the atmospheric global average is 421 parts per million (ppm) while by an open window at Al Aqsa Hospital it was 1004ppm.

Warfare damages the environment massively. The world's militaries account for approximately 6 per cent of all greenhouse gas emissions. Militaries consume enormous amounts of fossil fuels, which contribute directly to global warming. If the US military were a country, for example, it would have the 47th highest emissions worldwide. Bombings and other methods of modern warfare directly harm wildlife and biodiversity, which was why I was surprised to hear a dawn chorus, but there was one. The collateral damage of conflict can kill up to 90 per cent of large animals in an area. Pollution from war contaminates bodies of water, soil, and air, making areas unsafe for people to inhabit. I was seeing this in Gaza with its overflowing sewage. In the first three months of the war, the conflict produced 281,000 tonnes of $CO_2$, mainly from Israel's military actions, equivalent to burning 150,000 tonnes of coal. US cargo planes delivering military supplies to Israel contributed nearly half of these emissions.

Rebuilding Gaza's damaged infrastructure will further exacerbate the climate crisis. Thankfully, the UN has received an official request from the State of Palestine to undertake an environmental impact assessment but cannot do very much until the fighting stops. There is water pollution with up to 100,000 cubic metres of sewage and wastewater being dumped into the sea daily, which is the rough equivalent of 30 Olympic-sized swimming pools. There is debris pollution with likely over 45 million tonnes discarded since the war began, human remains still under collapsed buildings, asbestos in those same buildings, and almost a million tonnes of planet-warming gases released into the atmosphere. This is the equivalent of burning approximately 450,000 tonnes of coal, with 99 per cent of this air pollution being attributed to Israel's aerial bombardment and ground invasion of Gaza. Meanwhile up to half of all tree cover and farmland in Gaza has been destroyed, as have up to 62 per cent of all buildings.

Unexploded ordnance – approximately 10 per cent of all ordnance fails to explode – is also a problem with best estimates suggesting it will take 14 years to make Gaza safe, even should the war stop immediately. My measurement of substandard air quality at Al Aqsa Hospital was but the extreme tip of a very large iceberg. Gaza had a long haul ahead.

My ward round was its normal chaotic format. I started with the intention of seeing three especially challenging patients, each the result of explosive injury, to work out what I might do next. Before I had taken my first ten steps, I was surrounded by locals, each speaking so fast I could barely understand a word, and each waving a cracked mobile screen in my direction. Each screen sported an X-ray.

"Doctor! Doctor! It's my son – he is only 10 years old. Look at this X-ray. What can I do?" asked the woman, I would estimate in her late twenties, full black *burkah* in place. I glanced at the screen to see a broken upper arm bone (humerus), plenty of shrapnel, while the irregular outline of the soft tissues, which I could just make out on the X-ray, suggested the injury was open (compound). Infection was likely.

"Umm…" I replied. I was about to say that I should see the child when my local companion interrupted both my thoughts and words.

"No," he said. "We haven't the time. We need to be in the operating theatre in 15 minutes." He glanced hurriedly at his mobile screen as a text had just arrived. Then he looked at his watch, as if to emphasise the point. "Let's…"

"Doctor!" came the voice, this time a man. It was my colleague's turn to be interrupted. "It's my wife," the man said, his voice choking as he spoke. "They dropped a missile on our house yesterday evening. Our son was killed, and my sister is missing, but my wife hasn't been to the operating theatre yet."

I nodded and was about to explain when my local colleague replied. "We'll get to her soon," he said. "We had 70 casualties in yesterday, so we are a long way behind."

I saw the man nod and my colleague pick up pace, as he half jogged, and half stumbled towards the operating theatres. "Come!" he said, turning in my direction and making a beckoning sweep with his hand. "Let's get to the operating theatres and see what they have for us."

With difficulty I followed him, as we weaved our way through the throng of locals, each of whom wanted an opinion. As we rounded one corner on a staircase, I saw a group of five children, none could have been more than eight years old, each was silent but watching the two of us closely as we passed. They were holding hands with one another, each with an almost fixed stare. Within moments we were past.

"Tell me about those children," I asked. I tried not to sound breathless, but it was difficult to control my panting.

"Orphans," replied my colleague. "They have found each other and are sticking to one another like glue."

"How long have they been with you?" I asked.

"At least six weeks," said my colleague. "They were orphaned when there was an attack on Nuseirat Camp. Each of their parents was killed and they now have no adult to look after them, so they have made their home just outside the hospital and are looking after themselves. We are very worried by their mental health, but there are no mental health specialists available."

I nodded as we made our speedy way to the operating theatres. My colleague's response did not surprise me as I had seen the children's stare before, albeit in black and white photographs from the First World War. It was the so-called *thousand-yard stare*, the blank and unfocussed gaze sometimes seen in individuals who have experienced a traumatic event. In the First World War it was associated with what was then known as shell shock. Today we would call it *Post-Traumatic Stress Disorder* (PTSD). The group of five children showed that in spades.

Mental health was proving to be a major issue in Gaza, especially among the children who had taken an unfair share of the casualty load. Even before the war, a survey by a UK NGO, Save the Children, had shown that 80 per cent of Gazan children were exhibiting symptoms of emotional distress. That percentage would now be even higher. The distress could manifest itself in different ways – anxiety, incontinence, nightmares, and insomnia. It was then, and is now, a massive problem that will continue for a very long time. UNICEF had estimated that more than a million children needed mental health and psychosocial support and would have scars that will likely remain for life. There were also approximately 33,000 orphans in Palestine. I had just seen five of them.

Healthcare workers were also affected, and that included me. Many could not sleep as they thought that at any moment they might die. Or, if they fell asleep, they worried that they would not be able to react quickly and run away or protect their family. As I had discovered for myself, these workers were having to function under conditions that were inhumane and were experiencing anxiety, insomnia, depression, intrusive thoughts, emotional avoidance, and nightmares. Meanwhile Israel was persistently warning about an invasion of Rafah, adding pressure upon pressure. The Gaza war was a hotbed of mental health problems that I wagered would continue for several decades, maybe even longer, regardless of the outcome of the current fighting.

Some of the wounds I was seeing in the hospital were huge. In several cases they were the size of at least two outstretched hands, as well as being infected. There are various ways of dealing with such massive wounds, but a lot depends on the availability of equipment. One method is called Vacuum Assisted Closure (VAC). In this, the wound is covered by a plug of material that is cut to shape, the whole thing is then covered with material that looks like kitchen plastic, beneath which suction is placed through a thin tube and connected to a hospital's piped suction supply. This suction is continued full time, at various levels of power, and most wounds will slowly heal while infection gradually resolves. The VAC arrangement only needs changing occasionally. VAC is commonly found in more peaceful hospitals and is widely used globally. In Gaza? Sadly, it was not the same. There was one VAC kit for the entire hospital, no piped suction, few if any nurses to care for the VAC, and simply not the expertise to use it. Mostly, dressings were thus changed daily and that was it.

There are other, more traditional ways of encouraging a large, infected wound to heal. One is the so-called sugar dressing, and another is the use of honey. It is said that these substances were even used by the Egyptian Pharaohs and work by inhibiting the growth of bacteria. There is suggestion that sugar was used as early as 1700 BCE. Its use is counterintuitive, but the fact is that it works. For sugar, the same substance as might be used in the kitchen may also be used on a human wound. It is sprinkled over the full expanse of a wound and then covered with a dressing. Use a teaspoon if you wish, anything will do, as long as it is capable of holding sugar while it is being sprinkled. This must be done daily. The same applies to honey, with Manuka honey being best.

At Gaza's Al Aqsa Hospital, I suggested the use of sugar dressings, and emailed a former colleague with experience of this in conflict settings, although she was living in the Far East. She was helpful and encouraging, so based on her words, sugar dressings were accepted at Al Aqsa Hospital. There were plenty of wounds to heal.

There were 47 cases in the operating theatre that day, although there were many surgical teams involved in their management. In my peaceful UK practice, if I undertake five operations in a single day, that is seen as plenty, so Gaza was in a different league. Some cases were simple, others more complicated, but 47 operations were normal for Al Aqsa Hospital.

One of the cases with which I was involved required me to refashion and clean two above-knee amputation stumps, which had not been stitched closed but left open to allow any infection to drain out. The patient had been the victim of an explosion one month earlier. No surprises there. Just about all I saw were explosive injuries, from the first day I arrived in Gaza. Because a penetrating war injury was likely to be contaminated, a war surgeon did not close any wound, nor did they skin graft it, until any infection had gone. That could take a long time. The amputation stumps I was refashioning – a fancy word for tidying – required daily dressings but despite this they were still infected.

With the patient under general anaesthetic, which had been given by an anaesthetic nurse as there were insufficient anaesthetists to be present at each operation, I removed the dressings and looked closely at the raw amputation stumps. Gory for sure, but that is what war surgeons do. I could see signs of dead muscle and knew that once muscle was dead it will never recover and could act as a focus for the development or continuation of infection. There was also the risk of a truly problematic killer disease known as *gas gangrene*. This was common in the First World War. The only solution for the war surgeon was to cut out the dead muscle and keep cutting until there was only healthy tissue left behind. That is what I did, an operation that took a long time because both amputation stumps needed attention, each stump taking me roughly an hour. The room in which I was working was also tiny as it had once been a delivery bay but was now functioning as an operating theatre. I was unsure of its sterility. It would have surprised me if the place was truly clean as the inflow and outflow of patients was massive. Added to this were the many staff who would come in and out of the temporary operating theatre while I was operating, to use the single functioning electric plug there, in order to recharge their mobile telephones. Barely any of the staff I saw was wearing a surgical hat or facemask. The aseptic technique was appalling.

Having cleaned each amputation stump of its dead muscle, which essentially means surgically cutting it out, I needed something that would do a final clean. For that I used the so-called "Brown Bubbly" which was a mixture of hydrogen peroxide and iodine. Once squirted on a wound it fizzes, hisses, and bubbles, with the wound looking spotless within moments. This material was no longer used back home, but in Gaza was cheap, easily accessible, and effective. There was something about Brown Bubbly that made an operation feel excellent. The cleanliness of a wound after Brown Bubbly has been used can be truly exceptional.

Despite the news carrying claims that Israeli troops were withdrawing, the sky was still filled with *zinnanah* and I could hear their buzz almost wherever I was. When the hubbub in the operating theatres settled, and that did not happen often, I could even hear the *zinnanah* then, despite me being indoors. The IDF was promoting the creation of a new drone squadron, which may have been why the skies were so busy.

Meanwhile, if there was ever any doubt about the sturdiness of the Palestinian nation – never in my experience – a patient was admitted with a machete wedged firmly into the back of his right shoulder, a Palestinian-on-Palestinian injury. The casualty walked in the front door of the hospital himself and sat unperturbed in the Emergency Department while hospital staff busied around to arrange his slot in the operating theatre. He needed no painkillers whatsoever and never once made a fuss.

In Gaza, each day brought more death as strikes toppled buildings with families inside. Six months of war had killed more than 33,000 Palestinians, according to official figures, although I would wager the true figures, when eventually made public, will be considerably higher. Many of the buildings destroyed by Israeli attacks still had bodies of the inhabitants buried under the rubble. One Palestinian who worked closely alongside me throughout my time in the territory was almost in tears as he spoke of his childhood friend who had been killed five months earlier. His friend's body, plus those of his friend's family, had not been retrieved from the rubble that was once their home. The Palestinian agreed with my own observation that Israel had been picking off the more educated Palestinians, like Cambodia's Khmer Rouge did in the mid-1970s, to make it harder for Palestine to recover. The Palestinian felt that this was an attempt to eliminate the Palestinian nation, not just respond to the atrocities of 7 October 2023.

Israel's siege, bombardment, and ground offensive had created what the UN and aid officials called a man-made crisis of near starvation and famine. An impromptu tent city had now blanketed the edges of Rafah and was filled with hundreds of thousands of Palestinians who had fled Israel's offensive in other parts of Gaza. The influx had swelled Rafah to some 1.4 million people, approximately five times the normal population. Weeks of mediation by the United States, Egypt and Qatar for a longer ceasefire had been unable to make a breakthrough. Meanwhile international pressure was ongoing for a halt in the war while Israel claimed it was determined to expand its offensive to Rafah and uproot Hamas from what Israel said was its last stronghold. There was real alarm over a possible dramatic increase in casualties and an escalation in the conflict. My time in Gaza, rather than just hearing and reading about it from overseas, did nothing to make me more tolerant. I was seeing inexplicable injuries in clearly innocent individuals at least 50 times each day, sometimes more often. The war was a huge and intractable problem.

According to the few news bulletins I could access, Israel was meant to be withdrawing from my part of Gaza. You could have fooled me. The Palestinians had begun to briefly relax yesterday evening and I had listened to them partying outside while I had taken to an early bed. Wham! There was a huge explosion, which could not have been far away, and was sufficient to rattle my windows, blow shut my door, and billow the remaining strands of curtain. The Palestinian response? All they did was giggle. What chance was there of this war ever being resolved, I thought, if both Israelis and Palestinians were so minded. Gaza could be reduced to dust but still the conflict would continue.

* * *

# Chapter 11

# One Million Operations

I am not the best sleeper. I sense it is an age thing, so awakening at 4:30 a.m. Rafah time did not surprise me. What was unexpected, especially when faced with the news of an Israeli withdrawal, was the sound of heavy machine guns not far away, the loud explosions somewhere to my north, and the persistent buzz of an overhead *zinnanah*. For some reason I thought it might be quiet, especially as the Festival of *Eid al-Fitr* fast approached, marking the end of the Ramadan fast. However, Israel was still an aggressor and would not be disappearing in a hurry.

There was also a power cut, which took me a while to work out in the half darkness, although that did not deter the cockerel that I heard each morning as he heralded dawn. The morning chorus was getting underway, too, still a surprising feature of the conflict. Such things were supposed to disappear but apparently not in Palestine. I stumbled downstairs in the shadows from my first-floor bedroom, an unlit head torch across my forehead just in case. I preferred the dark, perhaps a leftover from my soldiering days. Darkness was quieter and more peaceful, and once my eyes had adjusted, it was easy to get around, while no one knew I was there.

I was also ashamed, as someone had clearly been in my small bedroom while I had been asleep and had removed several items so that they could make their own sleeping spot on a nearby couch. Normally, I would have awoken but that had not happened. Whoever it was had entered, rootled, and departed without me hearing a thing. They had left my door open, and some of my clothes on the floor, so I realised I had been invaded, but too late. Had they been Israeli Special Forces I would now be dead. I subsequently learned that the interloper had been an ex-Gurkha. He certainly knew how to move silently.

I finished my final ready-to-eat meatballs and pasta ration pack once I had reached the ground floor kitchen, so all that remained were three chocolate puddings, again ready-to-eat and in foil packs. I was not sorry about that as I was completely addicted to anything chocolate. Those in doubt are invited to check the glove compartment of my car back home. The meatballs and pasta ration pack was as annoying as ever, as its top never seemed to tear off cleanly, and remained attached while I ate the food cold. The result was that by the end of my prepacked meal, my hands were covered in pasta sauce, my fingers were stained brown, and I needed a proper scrub. The meal finished, I jettisoned the empty pack in a nearby overfull bin. As I did so, the power came back on. Fantastic, I thought. I turned on my laptop, now that power existed, but seconds later, there was a flicker, and the power went back off. It was going to be one of those days.

It had rained overnight, which was not unusual for Gaza. The territory had a wet season that lasted from early November to late March, when there was a greater than 10 per cent chance of rain on any one day. The month with the most wet days in Gaza was January.

The rain meant progress on the roads was slower, so my journey to Deir-al-Balah and the Al Aqsa Hospital took longer than normal. There were children out playing almost wherever I looked as they warmed up to the three-day festival and the end of Ramadan fasting, but it made driving even slower. We slithered around corners and twice saw other vehicles stuck in the mud. We were not allowed to stop and help.

The rain had made the sewage outflow worse, so we had to drive through the stuff even though it came halfway up our wheels. I kept the car windows tightly closed as the stench was horrendous. Meanwhile, and despite the deepening sewage, there was still a line of largely patient Palestinians waiting for their allocation of fresh water that was being distributed from a point immediately beside the sewage. It still escaped me why the IDPs had not experienced cholera. Perhaps it was something to do with Palestinian genes. Polio, typhoid, and hepatitis were also risks, in addition to gastroenteritis; indeed, any waterborne disease, especially those transmitted by what is known as the *faecal-oral route*.

The talk of an Israeli withdrawal had encouraged many of the IDPs to return to their homes, especially to Khan Yunis, which was only 9.59 kilometres (5.96 miles) from Rafah. I saw the returning Palestinians as they walked, bicycled, or clambered aboard cars and vehicles designed for half as many people as managed to find a handhold. For them, the claimed Israeli withdrawal was a blessing. Sadly, the Israelis thought differently, and many of the returning Palestinians were shelled and missiled back to their plastic tents, which were beginning to look more like permanent homes than temporary shelters.

Yet nobody could answer the one question I repeatedly asked. "What happens next?"

No one had an answer, other than a shrug of their shoulders. I doubted there was any better evidence to support the suggestion that the conflict was really a land grab by a stronger power, than the refusal to allow Palestinians back to their homes. There were numerous fine political statements saying otherwise made by politicians, but I believed few or none of them.

There was a bigwig visit to Al Aqsa Hospital today, from the Chief Executive of Medical Aid for Palestinians (MAP) alongside a senior member of a large US organisation, the International Rescue Committee (IRC). The Chief Executive had a streaming cold and did not look well. Unsurprisingly, I thought, as the pair had travelled a very long way to reach Gaza from Cairo and would be headed back in less than 24 hours. I now knew that journey well – it was not easy. Somewhere on the crossing of the Sinai Peninsula, perhaps on board a flight, the Chief Executive would have become infected. There were bugs in many places, so infection was hard to avoid.

To her credit, she avoided talking about her own clear discomfort and did not mention it once. I was asked what I thought about Gaza. "Look to the future," I replied.

"Tell us more."

"To focus on the here and now is clearly sensible," I said, "but there are so many big medical problems on the wards right now, and there will be even more in the IDP camps. Each casualty has multiple injuries. A single wound is uncommon. Most are infected, so there is plenty of surgery to come."

"How much?"

"One million operations would not be an underestimate," I replied, "even if the war stops today." I knew that one million sounded plenty, when in fact I believed it to be at the lower end of likely numbers. There was sufficient work in Gaza already to keep multiple surgical teams occupied for at least a decade, maybe even more. Surrounding me was tragedy, that much was clear. There could be no justification for the continuing slaughter and wounding I was seeing unless the aim was to wipe out a nation.

Stupidly, I tried to photograph the Israeli *zinnanah* today, the buzzing nuisance that spent all day circling overhead. There was no escaping it, as it went round and round over the hospital, probably at about 1,000 feet. It annoyed, yet fascinated, me too.

"There's your friend," would say the locals.

"No friend of mine," I would reply, wondering who was at the other end of the surveillance. I felt sure that was the role of the *zinnananh*. It just looked, looked, and looked again, reporting back to some senior rank in a foreign land who would decide if today was someone's final day on the planet. They could even be deciding about me.

I simply wanted a photograph to remember the occasion and I forgot for a moment where I was. Even in Gaza it was sometimes possible to feel relaxed. But I failed to think how locals might see this act, as to them it meant the hospital might be targeted. The fact that a bigwig was touring the hospital with a full photographic team and stopping in multiple locations for a photo opportunity, images that would soon be displayed globally, made no difference. I was a foreigner photographing a *zinnanah* and that was bound to create suspicion. After all, what would have been my purpose? The second I produced my camera and pointed it towards the sky I could hear a pin drop around me. Everyone within arm's length fell silent. I got the message instantly and pocketed my camera. If I had any doubt, seconds later an F16 fighter jet flew overhead. No missiles, no bombs but still someone was sending a warning. The *zinnanah* had spotted me and reacted, almost before I had time to think.

A major problem with living and working among Palestinians while warfare is waged all around is a natural increasing empathy with the Palestinian position. Generally, I am completely apolitical, even if I am required to take illogical but personal responsibility for the Balfour Declaration of 1917, which most in Gaza see as the beginning of the rot.

"It is your fault," said one, pointing in my direction and knowing my UK origins. Fortunately, I could see an understanding glint in his eye.

"It's not," I replied. "That was my forefathers. Anyway, they also said that Palestine should not be disadvantaged."

"They got it wrong," continued the accuser.

"Sorry," I would then say, apologising for the actions of individuals I had never met, more than 100 years earlier. It was not a time to argue. Had I done so things would not have ended happily. Yet that was humanitarian work. You carried the unsuspecting blame for all things to do with your country, whether or not you were the one at fault. Should a UK politician say something outrageous on the television or radio, from the comfort of their armchair, at the frontline you carried the can. In Gaza, according to the locals, I was partly to blame for all that was happening around me. Perhaps they were right, perhaps wrong, but I was not about to debate and argue. I was assured of losing, and changed the topic as soon as I could.

I found it hard to share so many of the Palestinian stories, each more tragic than the last. I worked closely alongside many of the locals, so it was common that I would hear their tales. One of my colleagues at Al Aqsa Hospital had his home demolished late yesterday, it seemed for no reason. The building was empty, and his family was thankfully away, so there were no casualties, but my colleague lost all his possessions, memories, and security in a heartbeat. I watched him closely. He was manifestly distracted but continued working and wanted no special treatment.

"Take the day off," I said. "Use the time to sort out the problem."

"No, doctor," he replied. "I will carry on working. I am just one of many Palestinians who have been treated in this way."

Meanwhile, another local colleague told me that now, despite me seeing life as terrible, it was a period that was the best since the October invasion. In those October days, he said, when he was in Gaza City, he was evacuated multiple times and even had Hamas firing rockets at the IDF only 30 metres from where he lived. He was glad to now be in Rafah.

"For how long will you be in Rafah?" I asked.

My colleague shrugged. "I don't know," he replied. "I have already moved six times, so why not a seventh or eighth?"

"Will Israel invade Rafah?" I asked.

"Most think so," he replied. "My friends consider that the invasion of Rafah is a political not military decision and that it will go ahead."

"Surely you can say that your offices are deconflicted?" I declared. "Then you will be safe." His offices were in the city.

"That is not true," replied my colleague. "Deconfliction requests, which are controlled by Israel, are only sent to the air force, not to the ground troops. There are no safe corridors for escape in Gaza and the Israelis will not negotiate such things. Should the IDF start a Rafah invasion, real chaos lies ahead."

My colleague was right. As I looked from the windows of Al Aqsa Hospital, to see the tents of at least 3,000 IDPs in the hospital courtyard, tents that were mostly filled with women, children, and the elderly, I could not envisage where the people would go if they were told to move once again. The same applied to Rafah city, not far to our south. A Rafah invasion would be a tragedy. Too many people in too small a space and nowhere for them to go. Israeli Prime Minister Benjamin Netanyahu had declared that the invasion of Rafah already had a start date. I did not know if that was true, or whether this was negotiation with one hand while holding a loaded pistol in the other. As a medic, the mere thought of an invasion was horrific. Al Aqsa Hospital already contained more than three times as many patients as it was designed to take. Increasing that number was inconceivable.

Ceasefire negotiations were continuing in Cairo and Hamas said it was reviewing the latest proposal presented by mediators in Egypt. Turkey had also issued an immediate export ban on Israel. Without any sign of let-up, Israeli warplanes had bombed homes in Gaza City's Zeitoun neighbourhood. In the previous 24 hours, 153 Palestinians had been killed and plenty more wounded. The totals were not looking good. Overall, at least 33,360 Palestinians had been killed and 75,993 wounded in Israeli attacks on Gaza since 7 October 2023. The Israeli death toll from Hamas's 7 October attacks stood at 1139, with dozens still held captive.

I found it strange that total numbers were seen as being important. First, I did not agree with any of the figures given, as I was sure the numbers were far higher. Second, every death and every injury was an individual tragedy for both the person affected and those around. Total numbers were irrelevant. One death was too many, irrespective of nationality.

I made a video today, to summarise my thoughts, and found a balcony overlooking the hospital's IDP camp where I could be undercover and not attract attention. I spoke for nearly eight minutes, away from the view but not the sound of the overhead *zinnanah*. My voiceover text went as follows:

*"I had hoped that visiting Gaza, and undertaking medical work there, might have cleared my thinking, and made it more evident why there is a war at all. It has not. It has served to confuse and concern me more. Even in Gaza I receive the details of fine words spoken by leaders around the world and yet I am uncertain if any of them have been here and seen for themselves the human tragedy unfolding. One glance, a blink, the briefest stare, and anyone with an ounce of compassion would see the great wrongs that are being committed on multiple occasions, each hour of every day. As I speak these very words, there is a drone buzzing overhead, explosions in the far distance and the sound of a heavy machine gun firing at something, I know not what. I do not believe anything is a mistake. It is my view that everything is intended.*

*Every day I make the one to two-hour journey from Rafah to the town of Deir-al-Balah and its Al Aqsa Hospital. There are temporary camps for what are called Internally Displaced Persons (IDPs) close to each roadside, indeed sometimes encroaching onto the road itself. The Palestinians are a mighty people, I have yet to find a weak one, and it is very clear that whatever may be done to them, their passion, their belief, their real sense of entitlement will not disappear. Gaza could be reduced to dust, indeed that is the situation in some parts, and yet the Palestinian spirit survives.*

*Each day as I drive, I pass the point where 24 hours before I entered Gaza, seven aid workers from World Central Kitchen were targeted and killed. Please do not say to me that their murder was anything but intentional. At least that is my view. Many organisations left or suspended operations at that moment. Medical Aid for Palestinians*

*(MAP), for whom I am presently volunteering, went the other way. For them there was no going back, and I totally agreed. I surreptitiously cross myself each time I drive past as I am never certain how Christian I should be in this heavily Muslim environment.*

*"What is going to happen to these people?" I ask my Palestinian colleagues, as I indicate the ramshackle tents each side of us, the children flying kites, the bartering over stolen food aid, the overflowing sewage, and the donkeys blocking our way.*

*"It is the question no one can answer," comes the reply. "If you hear something, please let us know."*

*I see tragedy around me, and it is not going away. Each of my local colleagues has been displaced and is living somewhere other than their homes. Each has lost friends and family. For some, bodies of good friends remain buried in rubble, for others the same applies to family. My organisation has been bombed, as have others, and only yesterday the Palestinian who supports me in my work, my local fixer, was told that his Khan Yunis home has been reduced to rubble. Another, a doctor from a nearby city who had been forced to flee to somewhere safer in what is this free-fire zone called Gaza, described being used by Israeli soldiers as a human shield. As the soldiers cleared his hospital, they compelled him at gunpoint to open the doors ahead of them and said they would shoot him if he did not. The doctor will take a lifetime to recover if he recovers at all. A volunteer needs serious empathy in Gaza. Sympathy is one thing, but it is empathy that is needed. Learn the difference should you decide to visit Gaza and be sure to have empathy in spades.*

*My hospital should have 200 beds and two operating theatres. Right now, it is housing 700 patients and has converted three delivery suites into smaller theatres to handle the load. It has given us a total of five operating theatres, one of which is kept free for emergencies. That theatre is invariably full. The wards have spilled over into corridors and there is no longer space for anything. Every day is a mass casualty day. Some patients have been in hospital for three months and the Emergency Department thinks nothing of keeping folk for 10 days.*

*The hospital tries to build and build, making space for the continuous arrival of patients. There is clearly a limit to what it can achieve. Conditions are harsh, equipment sparse, the few clinicians remaining tired and hurried, ward nursing unrecognisable, and patients much too close together. The result is many infections. Roughly 90 per cent of anything we do will become rapidly infected. Infection means a longer stay, a poorer result, repeated operations, and likely a life ruined.*

*I have only seen the injuries of warfare in Gaza, largely the result of explosions and mostly in children, women, and the elderly, with the occasional younger male. At least half of what I do is paediatric, and I spend considerable periods consoling families that have lost children. This is no coincidence. I see it as intentional. It is my third visit to Gaza, in as many hospitals, and in each I have been given freedom to roam. I have never once seen a tunnel, a uniform, or anything military. All I have seen is healthcare misery. I have asked many Palestinian colleagues, and they say the same. They, too, have never seen anything to suggest military activity.*

*When this is over, whenever the politicians decide, once they have ceased spouting fine but meaningless words, Gaza has much healing to do. One day perhaps the truth will out. Right now, I have chosen to believe nothing."*

Now that I have returned from the war zone, I read this text repeatedly, as it summarises what I was feeling at Al Aqsa Hospital, although I would perhaps correct the figure I gave for an infection rate of 90 per cent to make it 100 per cent. Infection was essentially universal. The footage was shot by a local who assisted me with much of what I needed to do. By the time I reached the end of my video, I saw a tear in his eye.

"You are crying," I said to this tall, strapping Palestinian, not the sort anyone might wish to cross.

"I am," he replied. "Every word you have spoken is true."

\* \* \*

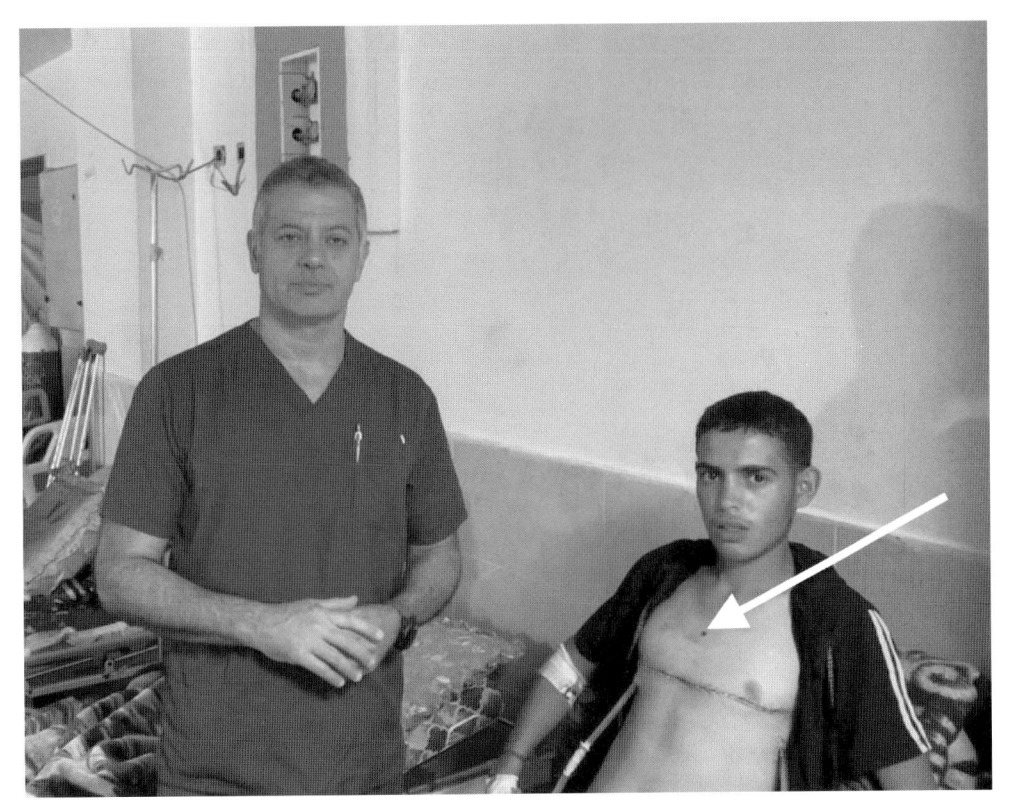

A small piece of shrapnel made that tiny hole – had it not been for the surgeon the patient would have bled to death. (*Courtesy of Khaled Dawas*)

Making a teaching video with a patient surrounded by a patient's family.

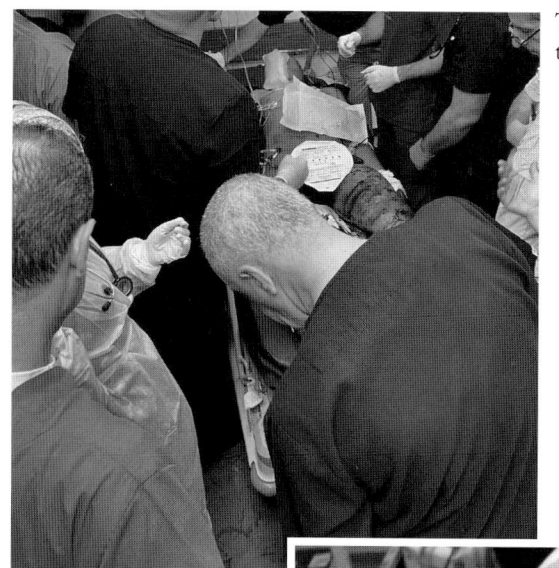

Teenage boy with multiple shrapnel wounds to his left thigh being resuscitated.

An amputation stump with a clean wound – almost ready for skin closure.

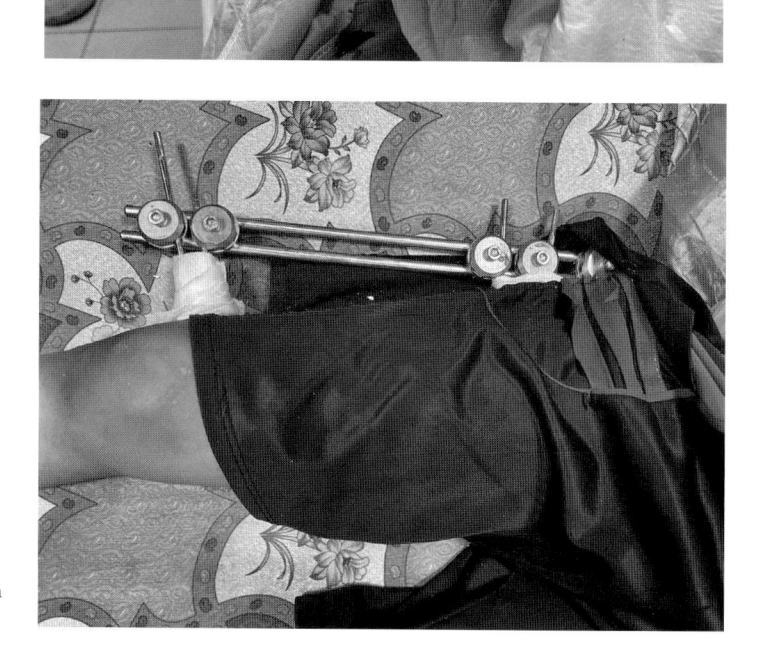

A child injured in an explosion and treated with an external fixator.

An elderly Palestinian woman, who has lost twenty-six members of her family, begs me to tell all of Europe.

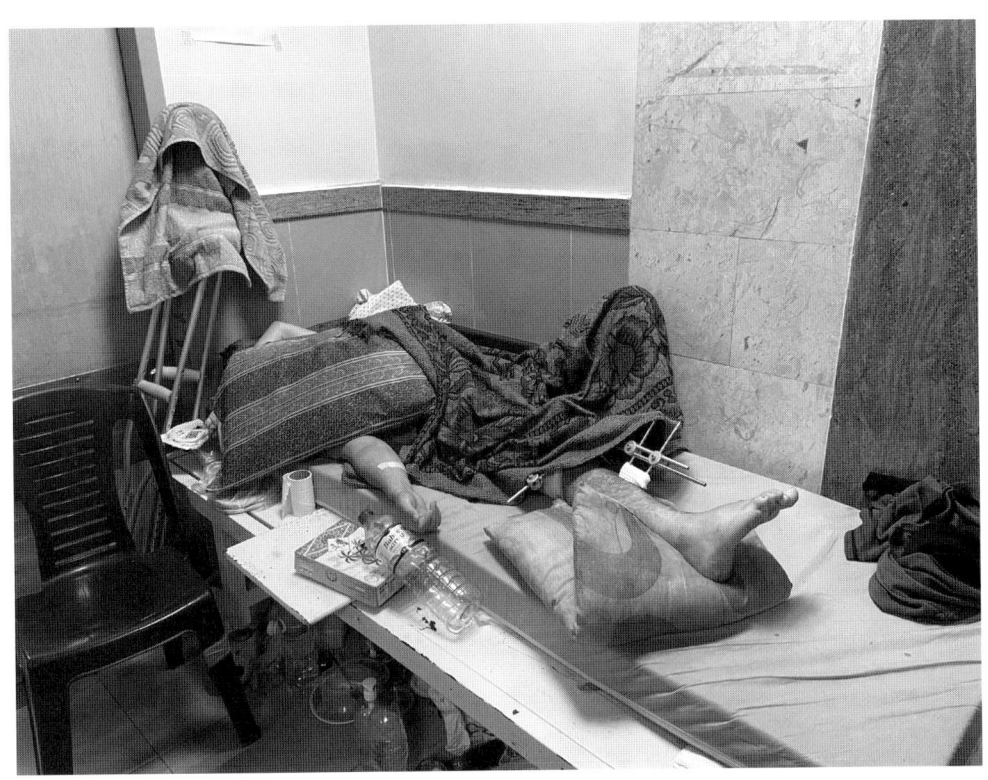

A patient seeking peace and quiet.

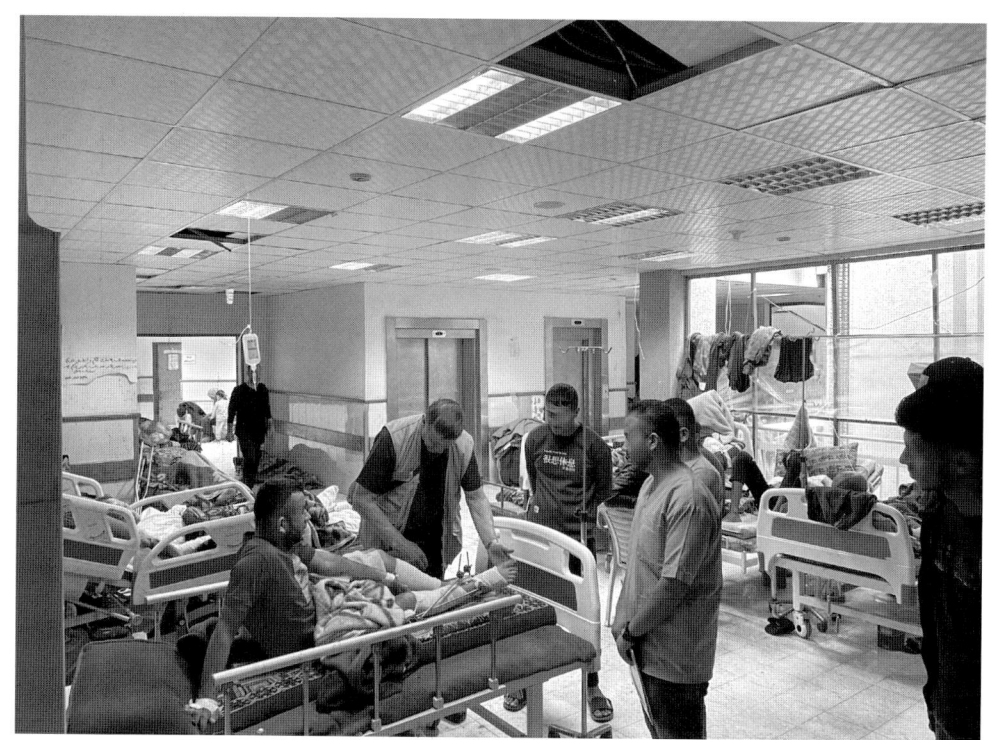

The author on a ward round.

No one in this photograph was being paid for their work on the ward.

My certificate of thanks.

The road to Al Aqsa Hospital – the seven World Central Kitchen aid workers were killed near here.

A sad Eid al-Fitr in Rafah – cloud, rain, and war.

A typical IDP camp, which was growing bigger by the day.

Rubbish seemed to be everywhere.

The ambulance drivers were incredibly brave.

Jostling for best position at a water distribution point.

Best place to find a signal even applies in Gaza.

The sewage just grew and grew.

Gazans heading back to Khan Yunis after an apparent Israeli withdrawal – the optimism did not last long.

Some say this was a war against children.

The golden sands of Gaza – prime real estate under attack.

# Chapter 12

# This Illogical War

It is time to confess, as my mission to Gaza had reached a high point in one respect but a low point in another. The good news was that I had finished my ready-to-eat meatballs and pasta, and all I had left was chocolate pudding. As a confessed chocaholic, being confined to chocolate pudding for breakfast was no punishment at all.

The low point was that it was Eid al-Fitr, a festival marking the end of the month-long Ramadan fasting. Traditionally, this should be a high point but today the situation was different. Eid al-Fitr traditionally begins at sunset on the night of the first sighting of the crescent moon and is celebrated for one to three days, depending on the country. It is forbidden to fast on this first day of Eid al-Fitr, and a specific prayer is nominated for the day. As an obligatory act of charity, money (*Zakat-ul-fitr*) is paid to the poor and needy before saying this prayer. There were plenty of poor and needy in Gaza. Traditionally, children are also given small gifts. As I drove to the hospital today from Rafah, in one of the IDP camps near the site where the seven WCK aid workers were killed, I saw a man in his 30s holding out a bag of sweets. A mob of children was almost crushing him, each shouting, "Me! Me! Me!"

Once again, I had awoken early to hear the *muazzim*, or at least a recording of him, blaring from the speakers that surrounded one of the minarets of the nearby Rafah mosque. I was a stone's throw from it. Added to the *muazzim* were the crowds, largely children, who joined in for the specific Eid prayer. There is no call to prayer on Eid al-Fitr. But I then realised there were no children – they were still in bed, or the equivalent in a plastic IDP tent. The children were also a recording. This was my low point. It was Eid al-Fitr in war. The *muazzim* was attempting to sound normal but was using a recording to do so. Yet the reality was different. Around me, there was little jollity to see. It was raining heavily, Rafah's dirt-track streets were awash, while a handful of sad adult Palestinians slouched up and down the street outside my window intently looking at their mobile telephones. I listened closely. There it was, the *zinnanah* somewhere high in the sky, making its unwelcome buzz. Eid al-Fitr was supposed to be a day of celebration, but events were conspiring to prevent that. The *zinnanah*, the occasional distant explosion, machine-gun fire, and the whoosh of a passing fighter jet. At least there was the regular dawn chorus of house sparrows, while the cockerel had no clue it was Eid al-Fitr and crowed until it was hoarse.

One of the many positive features of humanitarian work is that one's colleagues come from plenty of different lands. I have frequently found myself in the minority and Gaza was no exception. In Rafah there was a Pole, Tibetan, Italian, Jordanian, Pakistani, Indonesian, South African, plenty of Palestinians, and me. Each evening, when everyone tried to ring home, a process that depended entirely on Israeli cooperation by not interfering with the broadband, it was impossible to work out who was saying what. There were nine different nationalities speaking nine different tongues, and mostly very rapidly. I confess that I was probably the loudest.

This diversity of nationalities meant that tastes differed. For example, the Tibetan liked two tea bags in his one mug of tea, while the Pole could not tolerate powdered creamer in his coffee. Meanwhile, the Jordanian could not understand why I coughed and spluttered so easily when smoking a *shisha*, the Italian showed eloquence with just about everything, the Pakistani spoke perfect Urdu with a strong English accent, the Tibetan mumbled a mixture of slang Chinese and his own national tongue, and the South African used a corruption of Afrikaans. The best thing was not to listen to any of it, as when I did, I became rapidly confused. Humanitarian work is not simple and international tolerance is imperative.

Despite it being Eid al-Fitr, the Israelis clearly did not honour Islamic festivals as three hours into the day they had bombed properties not far from Deir-al-Balah and killed 30 Palestinians. They were simple targets, something the Israelis would have known, as families had come together for Eid al-Fitr. Bomb any building on that day and one could be almost certain there would be plenty of people inside it.

One of my colleagues saved a life today when a young Palestinian, somewhere in his mid-20s, returned to his bombed-out house to collect some belongings. He was targeted for being young, as he had no affiliations to Hamas, so the Israelis sent a missile into his house for a second time. The first occasion had been yesterday. As with many terrorist bombings, double bombs were used. The first begins the destruction, and the second waits until rescuers arrive to sort out the mess, or in this case, for the primary target to retrieve their possessions.

The boy, in some respects, was fortunate as he did not receive multiple wounds, which are generally common after explosions. He was wounded by a single piece of shrapnel. That was where his bad luck came in. The single piece of shrapnel, which was tiny, entered from in front, through his breastbone (*sternum*) and passed through the very centre of his chest. It did not emerge at the back and most likely buried itself in a part of the spine called a *vertebral body*. The vertebrae are unwittingly excellent at stopping shrapnel. However, in the process, the shrapnel made small holes in the Palestinian's heart and a large artery at the back of the chest, an artery called the *aorta*. A tiny entry hole in the casualty's breastbone gave no evidence of the catastrophic damage that had been created further in. The holes in the heart and aorta were minuscule, as when large they can kill a patient from bleeding out in less than 30 seconds. Blood came out of the hole in the aorta and headed towards the heart, building up under the membrane surrounding the heart, a membrane called the *pericardium*. As the blood accumulated, so the pericardium stretched until it could stretch no more, and the heart muscle beneath it became compressed by the gathering blood. Soon, the heart muscle could not work properly, and rapidly the boy began to perish. This gathering of blood under the pericardium is called *cardiac tamponade*. It was critical to act speedily, which is what my colleague did. From injury to being on the operating table took no more than 90 minutes. My colleague rapidly opened the Palestinian's chest through a long transverse incision just beneath each nipple, the holes were repaired, two chest drains were left in place to allow recovery, and the boy made it back to the ward. He was lucky to be alive.

    Mid-morning, for about 30 minutes, the *zinnanah* over the hospital fell silent. It would invariably worry me when that happened, as the peace and quiet would often be followed by the whoosh of an F-16 and the crump and thump of missiles or bombs. But on this occasion, it did not happen. The *zinnanah* fell silent, and two aid flights went past. They were lumbering Hercules aircraft, Queens of the Sky, that had completed aid drops into northern Gaza and flew over Al Aqsa Hospital on their way home. I was unsure from where they came. Aid drops by parachute made headlines, as they did look impressive.

However, the volume of aid they could deliver was small, and the falling aid was frequently dangerous, thanks to the failure of some parachutes to open or when aid was dropped in the sea. A 13-year-old was killed today by falling aid, not a good event during Eid al-Fitr. It was rare for there not to be accidents on the ground when aid was being parachuted from above. One aid drop two weeks ago killed 18 Palestinians. Twelve drowned in the sea while trying to collect the aid parcels and six perished in the stampede to collect aid that had landed on the ground. Parachuting aid to the needy was not a risk-free activity.

I was worried by the many children I saw in the IDP camps carrying lifelike weapons, even if they were only water pistols. The male Palestinian child would frequently ask his parents for a weapon very early in his life. If he did not receive one, he would find a length of wood and use it as a club. Fighting was deeply ingrained into him from an extremely young age. Unsurprising, perhaps, when most Palestinians had known nothing but violence throughout their lives. In our modern era, the water pistols looked like the real thing. With *zinnanah* overhead and children on the ground clutching lifelike water weapons, I worried that it would not be long before the Israeli in charge of the *zinnanah* would make a fatal misjudgement and a missile would then be launched against a child, who happened to be squirting water at one of his friends. Mistakes were made around the world on a regular basis, and I could see the same happening in Gaza.

On my ward round, I was astonished to learn that some of the staff in the hospital were not being paid, or were being paid at much-reduced levels. It appeared to depend on their employer. Those who were paid by the Palestinian Authority in the West Bank were still receiving a salary. Those whom the Hamas-affiliated Ministry of Health paid were receiving little or nothing for their efforts. I had not realised that so much of the work at Al Aqsa Hospital was being undertaken by either unpaid staff or volunteers. Without them, healthcare in Gaza would collapse. Within this same hospital, the difference between the two categories of staff, doctors in particular, was a huge problem and a frequent source of argument and debate.

A major problem of the war was the nearly complete absence of routine medical practice. Everything focussed on the war and there was little time for very much else. Yet life tried to continue, irrespective of the chaos around. I had seen many examples of neglected routine conditions that had been ignored solely because of the fighting. Today there were further examples. For example, I was asked to see a small neonate on the Special Care Baby Unit (SCBU) and was taken to a one-week-old child who was in an incubator. I looked at the child's X-rays and saw the multiple broken bones. The neonate had broken both upper arm bones (humerus), both thighbones (femur) and one shin bone (tibia). He may have broken more, but the X-ray quality on the proffered mobile was not good. The child had a condition known as *osteogenesis imperfecta* (OI). This is an uncommon, inherited (genetic) bone disorder that is present at birth, also known as brittle bone disease. A child born with OI may have soft bones that break (fracture) easily, bones that are not formed normally, and other problems. Signs and symptoms may range from mild to severe. The neonate on the SCBU had severe disease and had been born with his fractures. OI occurs in roughly 1 in 10,000 people worldwide and is even less common in this severe form. The condition often runs in families and the mother, who was in tears as I examined her new baby, told me that she had two other children in her tented home, and both had OI. It was quite possible, sadly, that the child on the SCBU would die within 6 weeks of birth. The poem Humpty Dumpty, so widely recited globally, is probably about a child with OI, and runs like this:

> *Humpty Dumpty sat on a wall.*
> *Humpty Dumpty had a great fall.*
> *All the king's horses and all the king's men*
> *Couldn't put Humpty together again.*

I could do nothing for the neonate, rather like Humpty Dumpty, and it was another occasion when I wished I had been able to speak Arabic better so that I could sit down beside the mother and talk quietly. I could not do that and was sure that sending a severe case of OI back to a plasticised IDP tent would be an assurance of the child dying in short order. Back home, a child such as the one on Al Aqsa SCBU would have been referred to the paediatricians and there was possible medication available that could strengthen the bones. None of that was available in war-torn Gaza.

Then there was the man in his fifties with cancer of the bladder and who was awaiting chemotherapy. There was none available in war-torn Gaza, so he simply had to bide his time on a list of 10,000 names, waiting to be evacuated out of Gaza for the chemotherapy he so badly needed. All the while he waited, his cancer was spreading. It would be touch and go as to whether he made it out of Gaza in time and, if he did make it, whether his cancer would still be treatable with chemotherapy. In the perfect world, you did not hang around with cancer but treated it as soon as possible.

Or the male adolescent with what was called *hyperhidrosis*. In recent months, his palms and feet had begun to sweat so that he was cold and clammy to touch. There were many causes of hyperhidrosis, and occasionally surgery was suggested to resolve the problem. However, the likely cause for this young man was anxiety – unsurprising in Gaza. His mother was a midwife and could understand some of my medical jargon, but the patient needed mental health assessment and regular medical review. Neither was possible in Gaza.

Many cases like these were gathering medical dust and could not be treated, thanks to a lack of manpower and facilities. I felt it was important that such cases were not forgotten. It was so easy to do so, such was the pressure on healthcare of warfare. Yet there was not much I could do except worry.

There was a school of thought that the Gaza war was actually a war on children. The Head of the UNRWA had said as much. One month ago, when the statistics for the first four months of the war were studied, 12,300 children had perished in Gaza during that period. That roughly matched the 12,193 that had died globally, from 2019 to 2022. Gaza was not a good place to be a child.

It is often presumed that a casualty needs one operation and that is it. No way. Multiple procedures are often needed over many weeks or months, even if everything goes to plan when the patient is first admitted. There are also those who can further injure their injuries, such as the patient who fell today as he was trying to walk near his bed. He had been admitted after an injury created by a missile several weeks earlier. An external fixator had been used to secure the fracture that the missile had caused of his left upper thighbone (femur). Unhappily, as he fell, he had shifted the position of the external fixator, and hence the fracture, so I decided to reposition it, which would need a further 60 minutes in the operating theatre. The anaesthetist decided to go to town and spent at least 40 minutes giving first a local anaesthetic injection in the patient's spine, followed by a general anaesthetic to keep the patient still. Meanwhile, the fresher war casualties were mounting up outside the theatre complex, as I needed to finish my procedure before the others could get in. Eventually, I found another pin and placed it into the upper thighbone, while securing the pin to the external fixator bar. The result was good, and I used X-ray control throughout, to be sure I had repositioned the fracture correctly. When I finished, the injured and uninjured legs looked identical, which was exactly as I had wished. Despite the anaesthetist appearing to take so long to give his anaesthetic, the procedure went well, and the patient was happy when he awoke. I can now only hope that the patient does not fall over again and displace my work. Sadly, in Gaza, anything is possible.

It is important to have peace and quiet in a hospital. It is a good thing for many reasons. Sadly, at Al Aqsa Hospital, the Gaza war prevented that. Even if the myriad of patients, families, and staff ceased talking, there would still be the *zinnanah*, in addition to the shells, missiles, and machine guns. Higher-level postoperative noise exposure has been shown to be associated with more severe postoperative pain, so reducing environmental ward noise might certainly help postoperative pain management. Florence Nightingale summarised the situation well, when she wrote in 1859:

> *"Unnecessary noise is the most cruel abuse of care which can be inflicted on either the sick or the well."*

My problem was that I had no idea how that might be achieved, as the wards were generally chaotic. There was a permanent background hubbub, with patients negotiating, celebrating, sympathising, arguing, crying, shouting, yelling, anywhere and at any time. Some patients tried to escape the mayhem by hiding themselves under their pillow. It was about the only way a patient could find solitude, and even that was imperfect.

I often found it hard to explain to non-medical people how huge the problem was in Gaza. I had bravely predicted to the Chief Executive of MAP that at least one million operations would be needed, and even that was likely an underestimate. To simplify the issue I had a brainwave one morning when I was undertaking a ward round. In any event, I needed to understand about Hamas fighters, as I had not seen a single uniform in Gaza and none of the patients looked anything like a soldier.

"Which ones are the Hamas fighters?" I asked my local colleague, as we picked our way carefully around the wards. Picking was an appropriate description as there were so many patients, it was sometimes impossible to find somewhere suitable to place my foot. Blankets would be strewn across the floor, and occasionally without me thinking, I would accidentally step on an outstretched limb, an event I only recognised when the patient squealed.

"There are none," he replied. "Every patient we are seeing was wounded inappropriately. Not one was holding a weapon."

"Do you have an idea of what we are seeing?" I asked.

My colleague shrugged. "They do not keep the figures," he said. "Before the war, we used to do that, but the numbers are so huge it would be impossible now."

"Let's do it then," I suggested. "How about a snapshot in time? We can record the next 100 patients we see and write down what is wrong with them. That should give us a good view of who is here and who is not."

"Good idea,'" my colleague replied. "We'll do that from now on."

And so we did. For the next 100 patients we saw, actually 110, we wrote down their age, gender, how they were injured, and, importantly, how many injuries they had. As I went around the wards, I had a clear impression that there were many injuries because of explosions and very few from gunfire. There also felt to be plenty of women and children and far fewer men than I would have expected.

The information took us nearly two days to gather, but the findings were fascinating. I was both right and wrong but what was undeniable was that Gaza had a long-term healthcare problem which would not be improving any time soon. Lots of people like me would need to visit the territory for at least a decade, perhaps longer, and even then, there would be persistent trouble.

For our 110 patients, roughly a quarter were aged under 18, and another quarter were over 35. The youngest patient was aged 2 years, and the oldest was 74. One-third were female, two-thirds were male, and more than half the patients had more than one injury. The maximum number of injuries for a single patient was five. Nearly 90 per cent were the result of an explosion; there were only 9 gunshot wounds anywhere on the wards and almost 96 per cent of the patients were there because of a war injury. Less than 5 per cent were there because of something else, while one patient had both legs broken because of torture. The wards were not a happy place, but this was true frontline war surgery with a seemingly endless supply of casualties. Gaza's healthcare needed help and there was no avoiding it.

This illogical war was still moving fast, and it was impossible to predict what would happen next. An Israeli air attack had killed the three sons of the Hamas leader, Ismail Haniyeh, in addition to several of his grandchildren. Meanwhile Spain's Prime Minister had openly stated that Israel's disproportionate attacks on Gaza were a world threat. US intelligence agencies had also concluded that Israel would not be able to destroy Hamas. From a war surgeon's viewpoint, this meant that there would be ongoing civilian casualties for a considerable period, while any Palestinian I had met appeared solely interested in peace. Never once did I hear war talk in Gaza, so I did not see Israel's logic in continuing the conflict unless it had an objective beyond the elimination of Hamas. That would not have surprised me. Gaza was now largely destroyed and would take a very long time to reconstruct. What Israel had done was destroy a land and ensure Gaza had no future. Unless it formed part of a Greater Israel, of course. Now that was a political thought and I am just a medic.

\* \* \*

## Chapter 13

# Gaza Could Be So Beautiful

I had hoped I would lose weight in Gaza. The worry, dashing and darting, unpredictability, near misses, and the evident shortage of food and water would each conspire to make me lose weight. Yet somehow, I seemed to be chubbier. I knew this because I was issued five pairs of theatre blues, the clothing surgeons wear during operations, when I had first arrived in Cairo. The blues were excellent quality but had two external pockets on the trousers. For my blues back home, these external pockets did not exist. Initially, filling the pockets was not a problem. Now, when I filled them with various items, including my mobile telephone, I could barely bend over, let alone squat. Next would come a tearing sound when I inadvertently crouched, and I would be fully exposed in this strictly Muslim environment. Shamefully, I then decided to carry a spare pair of theatre trousers in my grab bag, the small quantity of essential equipment I kept beside me in the event I had to abandon everything and dash. The grab bag was a constant requirement in war zones and I had carried mine in many locations, even when back home in UK. Now, to the list of essential items in a grab bag, I had to add a spare pair of surgical trousers. I cannot imagine anyone agreeing with me, other than a chubby fellow surgeon.

The war was having a profound effect on everyone and everything it impacted. The significance for public mental health was huge. One method of dealing with such pressure was to keep a war diary and I had met several Palestinians who had done that. The fancy medical description is Written Exposure Therapy (WET), as it was a means to find a new way to think about a traumatic experience. Writing about what one was thinking and feeling during a specific event was one way of helping relieve the symptoms of Post-Traumatic Stress Disorder (PTSD).

What about PTSD and how likely is it? I put myself through a PTSD questionnaire and established that I was experiencing symptoms that were of a high to severe impact and I should seek assistance straight away. Perhaps my daily diary was a way of controlling symptoms. I do not know the answer to that, but it appears that I think I am better than I am. The questionnaire I answered was the Post Traumatic Stress Disorder Checklist (PCL-5) and carried the following 20 questions. It barely took two minutes to complete. The questions, each of which needed a tick-box answer of "Not at all, A little bit, Moderately, Quite a bit, Extremely", were as follows:

1) *Repeated, disturbing, and unwanted memories of the stressful experience?*
2) *Repeated, disturbing dreams of the stressful experience?*
3) *Suddenly feeling or acting as if the stressful experience were actually happening again (as if you were actually back there reliving it)?*
4) *Feeling very upset when something reminded you of the stressful experience?*

5) *Having strong physical reactions when something reminded you of the stressful experience (for example, heart pounding, trouble breathing, sweating)?*
6) *Avoiding memories, thoughts, or feelings related to the stressful experience?*
7) *Avoiding external reminders of the stressful experience (for example, people, places, conversations, activities, objects, or situations)?*
8) *Trouble remembering important parts of the stressful experience?*
9) *Having strong negative beliefs about yourself, other people, or the world (for example, having thoughts such as: I am bad, there is something seriously wrong with me, no one can be trusted, the world is completely dangerous)?*
10) *Blaming yourself or someone else for the stressful experience or what happened after it?*
11) *Having strong negative feelings such as fear, horror, anger, guilt, or shame?*
12) *Loss of interest in activities that you used to enjoy?*
13) *Feeling distant or cut off from other people?*
14) *Trouble experiencing positive feelings (for example, being unable to feel happiness or have loving feelings for people close to you)?*
15) *Irritable behaviour, angry outbursts, or acting aggressively?*
16) *Taking too many risks or doing things that could cause you harm?*
17) *Being "superalert" or watchful or on guard?*
18) *Feeling jumpy or easily startled?*
19) *Having difficulty concentrating?*
20) *Trouble falling or staying asleep?*

I had only been in Gaza for a relatively short time and was judged by this PCL-5 questionnaire as being at very high risk of PTSD. I could not imagine how a local Palestinian might score, but I would wager they would be worse than me.

Telling the history of the war and getting the story out for others to hear was evidently a problem in war-torn Gaza. More than 100 journalists and media workers had been killed in the first six months of the war, and plenty had difficulties in having their written works published overseas. Gaza had been shown to be a location of extreme risk for anyone wishing to publish about what they did, yet there were still plenty of Palestinians who wished to tell the world what was happening.

Photographs of patients were a good example. Normally, I never show a patient's face in a medical photograph. It is not needed anyway. At the time of taking a photograph, I would immediately show it to the patient, so they could see that I was only interested in their condition, while their identity was inconsequential. However, at Al Aqsa Hospital, I was frequently asked by a patient to be sure to include their face, not to hide their identity. The patient wished to spread the word and saw me as a means to achieve that. For photographs of children, the mothers would often look at my efforts, say they were unhappy with the result, and ask me to take another, and another, and another, until they were satisfied their child's photograph could find its way onto the global media. Remarkable.

I had identified two sets of war diaries, both from very educated Palestinians. Both were good, but not in a form ready for publication. More work needed to be done. The diaries looked more like WET than text for publication. Some of the photographs I was shown were heart-rending. The daughter who had died, the mother who was missing, the brother who had been taken prisoner by the other side and had not been heard from for the past three months. It was difficult to know what to say. I did my best but felt certain I was wanting. Here is one entry from a Shams Khalil that stopped me in my tracks. I have made very tiny edits:

*"Troops have withdrawn from the blocks behind where I shelter, and residents were able to enter the area and check on their homes and*

*belongings. A friend of mine went to check on the status of his home, but when he reached the building, he could not enter it as he found a group of thieves armed with knives occupying the building and threatening him to leave. Sadly, this is not the first time I have heard such a story. Robbery has become common, and some stories reported physical assaults on people who try to stop it or ask for their belongings back. The current offensive has exposed the worst in people. Hunger has pushed them to steal aid trucks and sell them on the market at expensive prices and now they justify horrible actions and violence in the name of need.*

*My friend has shown me footage of where the troops have withdrawn. The mass destruction is unspeakably terrifying. I can say that tanks and warplanes have spared no building. The same as they did in Gaza City, my hometown. The current offensive has so far left no home for us to return to and yet made us think that ending this war would bring no change but a nonsense. Such are my thoughts when I am negative and weak."*

There was clearly an escalation taking place near the hospital as one of the Palestinian camps, Nuseirat Camp, just outside Deir-al-Balah, and roughly three kilometres away, was being attacked. Although three kilometres may sound nearby, it is a very long way in Gaza. It was claimed by the Israelis that the fighting was based on precise intelligence and undertaken by the IDF's Nahal Brigade, supported by the Israeli Air Force from the air and Israeli gunboats off the coast striking targets on the coastline of Central Gaza. I could hear many explosions from many different directions. The Nahal Brigade is one of the main Israeli infantry brigades. Its soldiers wore light green berets which had earned them the nickname "sticklights". It was their chief of staff, Nochi Mandel, who was dismissed after the deaths of the World Central Kitchen aid workers. Anything was possible with the Nahal Brigade, I thought.

I had been receiving reports of complete destruction of buildings in the northern part of Nuseirat Camp as the Israelis made their way through. It is worth defining what Gaza meant by the word "camp" The current war had displaced a huge number of people and they had set up their homes in different locations, but mostly in temporary camps, similar to a European campsite, and using materials and tents generally provided by charitable donations. However, there were also more permanent so-called camps, which consisted of many houses and apartments that had been made from brick and concrete. They did not look like camps, in the true sense of the word, and more like crowded townships. However, they were still camps, as they were filled by displaced Palestinians, but displaced by former wars, not this one, the one that started after 7 October 2023. Nuseirat Camp, for example, had its own mosque and was named after the local Nuseirat tribe. Most of its inhabitants came from the southern areas of Palestine, such as Beersheba and the coastal plain. Before the camp's establishment in 1948, its roughly 16,000 original population settled in the grounds of a former British military prison on the site. Nuseirat Camp had been home to many Palestinians for several decades.

Meanwhile, thanks to the Israeli assault on Nuseirat Camp, the air was filled with the sound of ambulance sirens as one casualty after the next arrived in the hospital's Emergency Department and went from there to the operating theatres. I could almost feel the workload increasing. The noise levels rose, there was a total lack of chit-chat, and people walked faster while determination was etched on their faces – it was manifestly time to focus on the priorities at hand.

Today there had been scheduled 31 dressing changes and 12 operations, but everything was put on hold because of the influx of emergencies. I managed to deal with three dressing changes before the final postponement of all non-essential procedures, as the full five operating theatres, three of which were only temporary anyway, were readied for emergency use. Cases were pouring in, mostly children, and the local staff were worried. Some had packed their own bags already, prepared for evacuation. This was the first ground operation carried out by the Israeli Army on the Nuseirat Camp since the war began, so events had to be watched closely. When the locals worried, so did I, and I thought it was time to notify Security, which I did, as I suspected I was a hair's breadth away from being evacuated, as was the full Emergency Medical Team.

The *zinnanah* continued to fly overhead, there were loud explosions nearby, and the sound of heavy machine-gun fire that I suspected was from Israeli tanks was clearly audible. There was a constant stream of ambulances arriving at the hospital. Israel was intensifying its assaults on many things, including aid convoys, as a UNICEF convoy had been attacked, too. There had also been attacks to the south and east of Rafah, so I hoped the one route remaining on which I could escape was not about to be cut off. Israeli civilians were also blocking the access of food for the Palestinian people by obstructing some of the aid crossings – Nitzana and al-Ajwa – between Israel and Egypt, so events were not looking good. However bad I may have thought the situation was, and it was truly appalling, added to the proximity of Israeli forces, the local doctors said the situation was five-star compared with earlier. Astonishing.

Worrying that I might have to leave the hospital at any moment, I made two training videos for teaching any surgical teams that were scheduled to arrive after me. The two patients I chose were astonishingly cooperative and did not worry in the least about their faces being shown on video to the world. My aim was to describe the differences between peacetime surgery, such as I had back home, and war surgery. There were huge differences, as these pages show. I also noticed that my local assistant was no longer dressed in dark blue, but light grey, so there was no mistaking him for a militant, as he was evidently preparing for trouble.

"I am worried about my parents," he said.

"Why?" I asked.

"Their house is still standing but they have nowhere to go if the Israelis destroy it."

My assistant's family home was barely five kilometres to the south of Al Aqsa Hospital and the Israelis were coming in from both north and south. Some of the locals were saying this was the beginning of a pincer movement. One from the south, one from the north, and meeting roughly where I was sitting. That did not sound comfortable.

"All we can do is hope," I replied. It seemed such an inadequate statement.

"And pray,' said my assistant, who also happened to be a *haafiz*, and knew every word of the Quran, from its beginning to the very end.

"And pray," I repeated. Again, this was an inadequate statement, but I felt it was the only one possible.

My assistant's mother had also sent me a small gift, which her son handed across to me. "You had best take this now," he said, "as I suspect we could be leaving in a hurry." He then handed me a small plastic bag that contained an old halva pot, the halva eaten long ago, and the pot now filled with homemade Palestinian biscuits. "These are *kaak asawer*," he explained, "traditional Palestinian biscuits that are filled with a date paste and shaped into rings. I bet you will love them."

"Thank you," I said, taking the small present in my hands. Outside, the crumps and thumps were going crazy. "I am sure I will adore them," I added.

I then looked at the small plastic bag neatly tied in a bow around the old halva pot. Everything was at a premium in Gaza, including old halva pots. "Would your mother like this pot back when I have finished the biscuits?" I asked.

My assistant hesitated for a moment and then replied. "No need. We can find another pot if required. You keep it."

I nodded, but even rubbish had its uses in war, and I realised that. The gift had a profound effect on me. It was not only that my assistant's mother had taken the trouble to cook and prepare something for a foreigner she had never met. It was also the care and attention to detail she had used when wrapping up the biscuits. It was the sign of an individual with high standards. Perhaps far more than my own. The tiny gift, which turned out to be delicious, was a sign of a great civilisation, now struggling for survival.

After the gift was handed over, we went to the operating theatres to help with what we could, but it was soon time for me to return to Rafah. The hospital staff were still on edge, wondering if they would soon have a hospital at all. The Israeli record of caring for healthcare facilities was not good. Yet by the late afternoon, the fighting in Nuseirat Camp started to settle, and I realised that there was a likely limit to the Israeli advance. It was probable there would still be a hospital standing by the morning. It would thus be sufficiently safe to return to Rafah, which I needed to reach before nightfall.

My drive south to Rafah was remarkably clear, I sensed because the fighting at Nuseirat Camp was audible to all, so many people had taken to their temporary shelters to wait for the fighting to finish. As we drove, sadly, I could see some evidence of animals being treated badly, mostly mules and donkeys. There were two camels as well. All the animals looked unhappy, and their body language was atrocious, although I cannot pretend to be an expert on such things. The animals just looked sad, and the local Palestinian who was driving me regularly reported that the animals were treated cruelly on a regular basis. Kindness was in short supply. There were also fishermen out at sea on their two-person paddleboards, which they used for positioning their nets, and other fishermen on the beach pulling in their nets. I did not see many fish flapping in the mesh. The fishing method looked to be *purse seine* fishing, which is when a fishing net hangs vertically in the water thanks to weights being attached along the bottom edge and floats along the top. Another technique I saw being used was *beach seine*, where the seine net was operated from the shore. A seine net differs from a gillnet, in that a seine net encloses the fish, whereas a gillnet directly snares them.

Once again, and despite the fighting being so near, I looked at the beach and sea as we drove south from Deir-al-Balah to Rafah.

Both off the coast and beneath the occupied lands of Palestine, over three billion barrels of oil were estimated to exist. To put such a huge quantity in true perspective, Saudi Arabia had even more than this, of the order of 267 billion barrels. There was also Gaza Marine, a natural gas field 36 kilometres (22 miles) off the coast, located in water at a depth of 610 metres (2,000 feet). The field was discovered in 2000 and contained more than one trillion cubic feet of gas, sufficient to power the Palestinian territories, added to the potential for some export. Compare that with Qatar, however, which had 858 trillion cubic feet of gas available. Although the Palestinian energy supplies were small when compared with many other countries of the world, they did exist and might also have been a cause for argument, maybe even war.

A constant feature of the area, and forever becoming bigger, were the piles of rubbish that were to be found just about everywhere in the IDP camps, at crossroads and street corners, and occasionally filling the shrinking open pieces of ground, shrinking because each day yet more tents and temporary shelters from somewhere would arrive. Each morning, I would see children scrabbling through the piles of rubbish, doing their best to avoid broken glass and toxic waste, as they collected scrap metal and plastic that might be sold to earn a living. By 9 a.m. the children would have gathered whatever they felt was suitable and the rubbish would then lie abandoned until the late afternoon. Then it was the turn of the donkeys that would seek scraps suitable for eating. Neither the children in the mornings nor the donkeys in the afternoons found much in the piles of rubbish, but each occasionally found something to justify their unsanitary efforts.

\* \* \*

# Chapter 14

# The True Leader

Something was going on in Rafah, but I had no idea what it might be. However, in the early hours of the morning, for the first time since I had arrived, the cockerel beat the drone to welcome in the new day. I supposed it was not too bad to be awoken by a cockerel in a war zone, as I normally heard the buzz of the *zinnanah* throughout the night and easily into daylight. But not today. To the north I could still hear explosions, likely near my hospital, as the Israelis were still battering Nuseirat Camp, barely three kilometres from where I worked. I would know more once I reached Al Aqsa Hospital in Deir-al-Balah, assuming the road was clear.

Then suddenly the reason for the *zinnanah*'s silence became clear. "Whooomp!" I jumped at the sound when I should have been accustomed to it by then. I must have heard at least 200 explosions since my arrival in the territory, likely plenty more. This new one was hardly new or unexpected. I controlled my involuntary response rapidly. A shell or missile had landed, fired from somewhere and something, although a jet was unlikely as I had not heard its whoosh. Although the sound was loud, and my tatty curtains billowed slightly, the explosion sounded to be well to my east, so I had not been the target. At least that was something to welcome, I thought, even if the explosion was bound to mean more innocents had been killed or injured. It was evidence, however, that the Israelis were having a go at Rafah and matters could only become worse, not better.

The drive from Rafah to Deir-al-Balah was more nerve-wracking than normal, thanks to the fighting getting nearer and Rafah now being firmly in the spotlight. I saw several smoke plumes rising to our east as we drove north, and I could sense the local people were jumpy. There were fewer Palestinians out and about and the children were less boisterous. Most of those I saw around me were displaced and eking out their livings in temporary shelters. A few of the more fortunate were either residents of Rafah City, and had long been that way, or had managed to find shelter in something made of brick. They were in the minority. For most of the displaced, it was not a single displacement, for they had moved multiple times. I had no idea how any population could tolerate this. It would be impossible to do anything but survive, and even that would have been a struggle.

As we drove north, I could see more tents being put up on either side of us and right along the coast. I guessed this was thanks to the threat of an Israeli attack on Rafah, so the local Palestinian population was getting itself prepared, and trying to find the best spots for a tent. There was no central organisation for allocating space. It was first come, first served, and anywhere would do. Eventually, there would be no space left for anything, which I sensed might be the problem in the event Rafah city had to be evacuated. The inevitable result of evacuating Rafah would be Palestinian-on-Palestinian conflict, which had already started, not just conflict with Israel.

Some Palestinians had anticipated this and placed their tents as close to the sea as possible. I worried about what might happen during a storm or spring tide. Perhaps I was worrying unnecessarily, or perhaps the desire for privacy – seashore tents were certainly very private – overcame any theoretical disadvantage. It was certainly a fine judgment to place a tent sufficiently near the sea but not too near. Get it wrong and you could be drowned in the middle of the night, or a fellow Palestinian would set up home beside you, or even between you and the sea. Get it right and you had almost complete privacy.

Work started early in the hospital, thanks to two children with abdominal shrapnel wounds, who needed emergency surgery. A third child was on the way. The threesome had been sheltering in a school in Nuseirat Camp, but naval shelling had destroyed the school, injuring them in the process. I could see why some saw this as a war against children. There was no possibility the three youngsters could have been anything other than innocent and no logic in shelling a school. Clearly, someone else thought differently. Alongside the children other casualties also arrived while explosions continued near the hospital. The fighting was certainly getting closer, and I could see my colleagues' bags were still packed in the event they needed to escape. There were filled bags in various corners of the hospital, behind reception desks, or under chairs. Many staff were prepared to run but were not going to declare that openly. The Palestinian way was to seem relaxed about the conflict but to move very fast if required.

There was one patient who was worrying me greatly. A man in his mid-thirties, he had been caught in an explosion some six weeks earlier. At the time it had been thought that an above-knee amputation of the leg was the only solution. Leg amputations come in various forms, the principle generally being that the longer the stump can be left, especially if below knee, the better a patient will eventually walk, assuming there was someone nearby who could manufacture artificial limbs. That someone was called a prosthetist, but there was no prosthetist at Al Aqsa Hospital. An above-knee amputation was fine, but the functional result for the patient would not be as good as if a below-knee amputation had been performed.

An above-knee amputation was duly undertaken, and the surgical team decided to suture (stitch) the stump closed at the same time as the tissues looked healthy and clean, so that all the skin had to do was heal. That was the start of the patient's problems. I learned long ago that to suture closed any wound created by a war injury is a gamble. Almost all will become infected, especially those created by an explosion. There is so much dirt and grime stirred up by the incident, some is bound to find its way into the wound. For this reason, I leave all war wounds unsutured when I see them for the first time. Cleaned yes but sutured no. It is only later, sometimes many operations later, that I do what is sometimes called a *delayed primary closure* (DPC). A DPC had not been done for this patient, as the wound had been primarily sutured, so five days after his injury his sutured stump became infected, and the stitches had to be removed. There was no point in putting them back in until the infection had settled, and that was taking a very long time to achieve. The patient was thus scheduled for a change of his dressing every day and under general anaesthetic, but even with that, the amputation stump looked infected, and it was not possible to suture it closed. On one occasion, I tried to cut away (excise) more infected muscle, but even that had not worked. It meant that the patient had received more than 30 general anaesthetics and was still no better. If anything, he was looking worse. Long-term chronic infection has been known to make patients extremely sick, and sometimes can even kill them. I was worrying what I could possibly do next, other than amputate the leg even higher than had already been done, and that seemed ghastly.

I was stuck, and so was the patient. I resolved to make no firm decisions but to talk with my colleagues to see what they thought.

It was helpful to work in a team, as with many of the patients I saw, there was more than one way of dealing with their problems. Talking the options through and hearing colleagues' thoughts, was very helpful for me and even more beneficial to the patient.

Now that I had been in Gaza for a fair length of time, the local people had begun to open up and tell me their troubles. None of what I heard was easy listening. Much suggested that this was a racist war, as if brother was fighting brother. I use the Oxford Dictionary for many things, so I looked at it online to find the definition of racism. It read:

> *"The inability or refusal to recognise the rights, needs, dignity, or value of people of particular races or geographical origins."*

Whoever said this was a racist conflict was perhaps not far from the truth.

One local colleague whom I greatly admired, as he was manifestly bright and intelligent, not only claimed that the conflict was racist, but told me his worries for Gaza. He did not feel the territory could take another six months of war as everything was deteriorating rapidly. For that reason, he had spent roughly US$60,000 to evacuate his entire family to Egypt and Jordan. Within the next two weeks his full family would have gone, and he would be the only one remaining. I could hear the tone of his voice as he spoke. Understandably he was highly emotional as he had no clue if he would ever see his family again. Warfare, just or unjust, is a tragedy for the innocent. It is bad enough for the fighters but a true disaster for the innocents. My colleague felt that all Gazans would do the same if they were able to afford it. His father has sold his car to make money for the trip and had taken a huge financial hit in the process. A car that cost him US$36,000, he sold for US$10,000 one year later, so desperate was he to leave the territory.

It appeared that Palestinians paying to exit Gaza was not a new phenomenon and was happening even before October 2023. As Israel and Egypt had imposed strict border controls to contain Hamas' rule in Gaza, the Egyptian Hala travel company offered regular fee services on Egypt's border. This was seen as an opportunity to get more dollars into the Egyptian market and was important as Egypt's economy was struggling, inflation was high and the country was desperate for dollars to purchase wheat and pay off its mounting debt. Since the start of the Gaza war, revenue from the Suez Canal had also plummeted, as cargo ships were avoiding it because of Houthi missile attacks in the Red Sea.

Although the fees for escaping Gaza were high, they were cheaper than earlier in the conflict. At the beginning of the war, those who paid to leave Gaza were merchants and business people, whereas after six months of conflict, few of them remained. Demand also fell because of the high prices, so these were lowered to maximise the number of travellers and thus the profits. There is always someone who makes money from conflict. Any war will show that. I was learning plenty by talking with locals.

Injuries from explosions carried many complications, and one was the loss of bone. The power of a blast clearly ruptured skin and peppered the hapless victim with shrapnel, but it could also blast a casualty's bone into oblivion. The bone could break, and frequently did, but it was rarely a clean break and was normally smashed into many fragments, something the medics called *comminution*. Comminuted bone could remain within the casualty, or it could fly everywhere at the time of the blast, and plenty could go missing, likely buried under the rubble of a collapsed building. Should it have done so, then large sections of critical bones could disappear. For war surgeons, that was when the hard work started, as not only did they have to stop any infection, but they also had to replace missing bone. Normally, in peaceful UK, this might have involved taking some bone from a casualty's pelvis, for example, and transferring it into any gaps, a process known as *bone grafting*. In Gaza, there was a problem with this, as the gaps could be so huge that a patient had insufficient bone of their own to fill the gaps created by the explosion. Another solution, albeit temporary, was to fill the gap with a material called *bone cement*. This could fill a gap and also be loaded with antibiotics to reduce the chances of infection. However, bone cement could not last forever and, at some point, would need to be changed for bone graft. Therein lay a problem. Unless a patient's own pelvis could be used, there was no bone graft in Gaza. It was a problem that needed to be solved once the fighting stopped and the medics were permitted to get on with what they did best – making patients better. With so many explosions in Gaza, there was plenty of bone to be recreated and many years of work required.

War surgery was not all about saving lives. It was also about administration. A problem of operating on so many patients in such a short time was that patients could easily go missing, as it was not possible to find a patient on the ward after surgery had been undertaken. There were simply too many casualties. The operating theatre was sometimes the only place a war surgeon might see a casualty. The rest was in the hands of the wards, and if they were understaffed or inexperienced, patients could suffer, despite the best efforts of the surgeon. It was thus important to write good notes to describe what had been done, the reasons why a particular decision might have been made, and how a patient should be handled afterwards. It was the only way of passing the message on to others and allowing continuity of care. Continuity was essential, as surgery was not a one-stop shop.

A major problem I saw was the healing potential of the casualties. Famine was already established in Gaza, so a wounded individual was weakened even before a missile struck. It was not possible to equate the recovery of a patient in the UK with the recovery of a patient in Gaza. The two would be wildly different. Problems that were tiny in the UK could become major in Gaza simply because a patient started off by being weaker. Infections were more common, healing took longer, and morale could easily flag. In contrast, family support in Gaza was so much better than at home, and people did truly pull together as a team. That could make a massive difference to the outcome but did not fully compensate for a patient who had been weakened by an ongoing war, famine, lack of water, unpredictable accommodation, loss of income, and so much more. It was one good reason war surgery was so different from anything else. Complex operations of any kind in a war zone could so easily end up in disaster. Keeping surgery simple was essential.

Another issue was understanding how the locals saw me. I knew how I saw them, but as the visitor, it was important to see things from their point of view. I was there for a relatively short time, but they were there forever, or for what might have seemed forever to them. It was important for me not to behave as if I knew everything, which I certainly did not anyway, and to involve the locals in all decisions. In the operating theatres, it was also best to assist rather than act as the first surgeon. During any operation, in any part of the world, there is the first surgeon, who carries the responsibility for everything, and a variable number of assistants helping. As a war surgeon on attachment, as I was, I would try to be an assistant and allow the locals to be first surgeons, yet I had to be ready to take over as first surgeon in a flash. It was important always to ensure that the locals were treated with respect, even if I completely disagreed with their opinion, and they could leave an operating theatre with their heads held high. They would be there long after I had gone home, assuming I could get home. Judging by the shells and missiles continuing to fall, getting home was not a foregone conclusion.

However, perhaps being a war surgeon in a foreign land is a good example of true leadership. To me, a leader is someone who encourages others to do what is right without them realising they are being led. That is the trick of being a war surgeon and is a skill that takes time to hone.

I was given a dilemma today, with which I had no idea what to do. One of the locals, whose property had been demolished by an Israeli missile a few days earlier, for no reason I could establish, had asked me to give him some money. This was to help reconstruct his property that was now lying in ruins, with much of his life and possessions scattered up and down a bombed-out street. He had been born there and had lived in the house all his life, but the place was now a pile of rubble. Ideally, he wished to have payment in US dollars. It was not a large sum by UK standards, and certainly a sum I could afford. Yet tongues wag in war zones, just as they do elsewhere, but perhaps more in war zones than normal. People see things and interpret them wrongly, and as the visitor, I had no escape. I had to rely completely on the locals around me. If a local asked me for something, even if instinctively it felt wrong, I had to take it seriously. I knew that if I gave the local the funds he sought, and even if I pledged him to secrecy, my donation would reach the ears of others within moments. There was no such thing as secrecy in war. Nor, for that matter, was there truth. The next stop would be me being asked for more money by others, and on it could go. The proper response was to decline, but as my life and safety might depend on this individual, I had to think carefully.

What did I do? Now that would be telling. It is up to you to guess.

\* \* \*

# Chapter 15

# Patch, Mend, and Save

I was mind-whirling last night and did not sleep well, so woke up shortly after dawn feeling terrible. It was one of the problems of being in a warzone. I had frequently woken up early worrying about everything and yet nothing. I was not worrying about my life, as in many respects that was already determined. If my Muslim colleagues were to be heard, I had no control over my future anyway, as it was in the hands of a far greater power than me.

In the early morning, as the cockerel crowed and the *zinnanah* buzzed, in the distance was the sound of a heavy machine gun, perhaps from a tank or possibly an Apache helicopter. I was not worrying about the sounds of conflict, but I was worrying about the Palestinian people. Those I had seen in Gaza exemplified the statement that one should never judge a book by its cover. I had seen owners of gymnasia that had been destroyed by war, yet they took pride in the welfare of the human body. I had seen IT experts who knew far more about technology than I could ever understand. I had seen medics with online consultation businesses, and I had seen images of magnificent Gazan seaside mansions with manicured green lawns and wonderful flowers. The eastern Mediterranean alongside which I drove each morning, from Rafah to Deir-al-Balah, was so attractive I wanted to dive in and take to its waters, yet an Israeli gunboat lurked angrily on the horizon, almost tempting me to have a go so that it could justify unleashing its fury. I am unsure if it would enjoy killing me for the sake of killing – I had seen plenty of that in Gaza – or whether its true agenda was to claim ownership of the fossil fuels that lay beneath the eastern Mediterranean.

My drive to Deir-al-Balah and the Al Aqsa Hospital was speedy, and paradoxically picturesque. The fishermen were out on their double paddleboards, and some were pulling in nets. The offshore waters on the coast beside me were quite shallow, which made them dangerous for the fishermen. The occasional one drowned but fishing was an essential job as it was one of the few sources of fresh food.

Yet each day as I had made the drive from Rafah to Deir-al-Balah and back in the evening, the sea beside me was the one that featured in the widely cited slogan, "From the river to the sea, Palestine will be free."

For a while I dared not ask about the slogan, as so many in the West had been penalised for doing so. It seemed a statement that would be best not to broach. Then one day, when I had been talking about this and that, nothing in particular, I blurted out, "What does it mean, that river-to-the-sea thing?" I asked one of my Palestinian colleagues. I knew him to be broad-minded.

"It depends where you are from," he replied.

"Tell me."

"It is a political phrase that says there will be one land between the Jordan River and the Mediterranean. Today it includes both Israel and the Israeli-occupied Palestinian territories of the West Bank and Gaza."

"Who would live in that land?" I asked.

"That is the question," replied my colleague. "The meaning of the phrase depends on who says it. Basically, both Palestinians and Israelis feel they own it when, in fact, neither probably does to exclusion."

"Oh," I replied, still not fully understanding the problem while silently thanking my Maker that I was a medic. It was better I stayed that way. At least I had asked.

The small cohort of Palestinian friends I was slowly amassing had told me that I should have seen Gaza before this war. It had been expanding, growing, and becoming wealthier by the year. Palestinians were proud of their Gaza, and only a few had the desire to leave. Now, the situation was different, and many were trying to escape. I sensed that may partly have been the Israeli objective anyway, to force the wealthier out, certainly if a land grab was underway.

What seemed clear, at least to me, was that there was plenty more to this conflict than one single nation versus another single nation. There was money behind all of it and agreements made between major powers of which most of us would be ignorant and with which many of us would disagree. I was glad to be a medic as I had long been a hopeless politician, but repeated missions to the Middle East over many decades, dealing with the effects of warfare, had forced me to understand a little. With Gaza, any solution to the Israel/Palestine conflict was beyond me, but when faced with many hundreds of casualties coming through a hospital's front doors, day in and day out, it was difficult not to ask, "How did they get here?" Anyway, until the fighting ceased, there was not much I could do, other than to patch, mend, and save as best I could.

The Palestinians had a deeply developed civilisation and were not just a desert people who should be overrun and ignored. There were many examples of their development and social organisation. For example, the Palestinian *hikaye*, a unique form of oral literature performed by women, particularly the older ones. In 2008, *hikaye* was inscribed on UNESCO's List of Intangible Cultural Heritage. Sadly, the tradition was slowly vanishing because of changing social structures and the spread of mass media. *Hikaye* were originally intended for entertainment and education and were mostly performed in a domestic environment, usually in winter. I tried to find *hikaye* in the hospital, but unfortunately there was none to hear, as the people were so focused on plain survival, which had usurped much of normal Palestinian existence.

Then there was Palestinian dancing, which I encountered on the first day of Eid al-Fitr, beside the beach at Deir-al-Balah. It was a *dabkeh*, 11 dancers in a straight line, grasping each other's shoulders, while smiling, dancing, and singing. It was remarkable, and similar to a Greek *sirtaki*. The *dabkeh* was a popular group dance in Palestine that was accompanied by traditional wind instruments and popular singing. It was a social activity and was performed in several regions during festivals, celebrations, and events such as weddings, graduations and, in this case, Eid al-Fitr. *Dabkeh* expressed cultural identity and is now on the UNESCO Representative List of the Intangible Cultural Heritage of Humanity. When I saw the *dabkeh*, I was unable to stay long, as there were spies everywhere and a *zinnanah* buzzing overhead, but to see such a traditional dance being performed in a war zone was remarkable. These people had so much to think about and so many worries and unpredictabilities, yet they still had time to dance.

To see these various aspects of Palestinian culture reinforced the view I gave six months earlier, when Hamas had done what it did in Israel, and before Israel had responded.

"What do you think will happen?" I was asked by a former UK military commander.

"They can reduce Gaza to a pile of dust," I replied, "but they will find it hard to eliminate Palestinian spirit."

I was seeing this in action. Down came another building, in came a dozen children with explosive injuries, but the Palestinian people still had time to dance.

I decided the spooks had tracked me down today, thanks to a WhatsApp telephone call I had with the UK two days earlier. Until then I had remained silent online as it had seemed the safest bet. Yet today, for the first time, my laptop computer misbehaved. I would press a key, and nothing would happen, or half the space bar worked well while the other half was dysfunctional. For some reason, the letter "z" was a problem, perhaps because it was the first letter of the word "*zinnanah*". I would switch the laptop off and restart it, and the keyboard worked perfectly. Initially I thought it was a case of *humus keyboard*, which is what happened when Palestinian humus – I had consumed plenty – sneaked its way under one end of a laptop's spacebar. On reflection, I did not think humus had anything to do with it but I had been spotted by the spooks and they had given me something nasty to discourage me in my work. They probably knew more about me than I knew about myself. My protection was being a medic, and following that course was no hardship, but it was critical that I did not wander. Non-medics did not understand medics – we were essentially a different species – so I had no wish for a spook to misunderstand me. If that happened, the next step would be a missile, and I was clearly not immortal.

The lack of medical equipment at Al Aqsa was worrying me badly as the only solution was improvisation and even that was becoming hard. The equipment shortage in the operating theatres had become so severe that it would have been laughable had it not been so serious. Just about everything was in short supply, so each operation was a matter of finding the next best item to use. Meanwhile, aid was having trouble getting through. For all I knew, a full storeroom of supplies was sitting in a stationary lorry on the roadside, somewhere between Cairo and the Rafah crossing. Israel was only permitting small quantities of aid into Gaza each day. Should it decide to close the crossing, which I guessed was likely in the event of an assault on Rafah, shortages would become shorter still and human welfare would fall apart, in addition to me being trapped in Gaza.

The stories from my local colleagues kept coming, and I was keen to allow them to talk. I was clearly in Gaza to be a surgeon, but a major part of what I did was listen. Empathy was important in such places, as was smiling. I am sometimes asked what the most important instrument for a war surgeon is. I normally reply, "A smile." If you have neither empathy nor smile, I suggest training before you leave home, even if you are the planet's most talented surgeon.

One tale I heard today was distressing. A colleague told me of a good friend who was living in a partly demolished house somewhere in Gaza City. This city had been home to 600,000 people before the war but 75 per cent of its buildings had now been damaged or destroyed. To this could be added damage to 73 per cent of Gaza's schools, the majority by direct fire. This destruction level was worse than that of Germany's Dresden at the end of the Second World War, when 59 per cent of its buildings had been damaged. Gaza worse than Dresden? I could barely believe it, but it was true.

My colleague, and I had no reason to disbelieve him, told me that in the immediate aftermath of the part demolition of his friend's house, Israeli soldiers caught his wife. Despite her evident pregnancy, and her telling the soldiers as much at the time, they raped her and forced her family to watch. How could that ever be justified? It could not.

There was so much destruction taking place around the territory that demolition was now seen as almost normal. It was the way war was being waged. The conflict was more than about people and fighters. It was about the land they inhabited, too. It appeared that the Israelis had demolished much of the northern part of Nuseirat Camp, only three kilometres from my hospital. I assumed they would do the same for its southern portion and then move onto Deir-al-Balah, where the hospital was located. Most Palestinians considered that Rafah would also be assaulted in the near future with an overall aim of making

Palestine so uninhabitable that its current occupants would be forced to leave. There would be little remaining anyway. At that point, in would come Israel and its allies, reconstruction would begin, and the job was done. Land ownership would have been transferred and the land grab complete. I could only hope I was wrong.

Once again, the cases in the hospital were largely very complex and well beyond what any hospital in a war zone might handle, certainly with such a high rate of infection. Basic surgery was fine, but the more advanced it became, the more likely it was that problems would intervene, infection in particular. The hospital staff and patients realised this. It was why most patients kept containers of antiseptic hand gel beside their beds. It was they who insisted I use it. I never had to ask.

Today, a volunteer male ward nurse told me as I did my ward round, "This hospital is contaminated." He was right.

I found it odd that the hospital knew of its shortcomings, both on the wards and in the operating theatres, yet little was being done to correct the situation. Perhaps it was the pressure of war. There was so much work that it was difficult to find time to do anything other than recover and wait for the next influx, which might arrive at any time, day or night.

Gaza was not a good place to be. Less than 12 hours earlier the Israelis had destroyed the Abu Bakr as-Siddiq mosque in Deir-al-Balah itself, not far from the hospital. This was one of more than 1,200 mosques that Israel had wrecked since the war began. In the last day alone its attacks on Nuseirat Camp had killed 19 people, in addition to wounding 200 others. Meanwhile, Israeli settlers had carried out multiple attacks across the occupied West Bank, killing one and wounding several Palestinians, burning cars and homes, and shooting at Red Crescent ambulances. Tensions remained high in Israel with its army on high alert for an expected attack from Iran. In preparation for possible Iranian involvement, the US had moved warships into position to protect not only Israel but its own forces in the Middle East. The view of the Palestinians around me was that although they would welcome Iran's involvement, they worried that it could divert attention away from Gaza and lead to further Palestinian displacement. They had a point.

Worryingly, there were reports from some of the IDP camps near Rafah that there had been more cases of waterborne diseases, for example gastroenteritis, especially while there was a lack of clean water and the territory was experiencing warmer weather. Contaminated water and poor sanitation are linked to diseases such as cholera, diarrhoea, dysentery, and hepatitis A, which are the last things that Gaza needed. The World Health Organization (WHO) had recorded more than 345,000 cases of diarrhoea, more than 105,000 of which were in children under five years old, since the war began. Gaza's only natural source of water was the Coastal Aquifer Basin, which ran along the eastern Mediterranean coast from the northern Sinai Peninsula in Egypt, through Gaza and into Israel. Approximately 90 per cent of Gaza's water supply came from that. The remaining 10 per cent came primarily from three Israeli pipelines and from small-scale seawater desalination plants. Of 581 key water and sanitation facilities, 37 were destroyed, and 226 had suspected damage within four weeks of the war starting. Daily bombardments restricted Gazans' ability to collect water, made farming difficult or impossible, endangered the staff who were operating the water plants, and limited the circulation of water tankers. Gazans' access to water from all sources, including desalination and external Israeli sources, quickly dropped by 95 per cent at the outbreak of war so that the average Gazan was soon living on only three litres of water/day for everything. The UN recommends an emergency standard of 15 litres. Consequently, up to 70 per cent of Gazans had resorted to drinking salty and contaminated water straight from wells and even that supply was declining. Gaza was in big trouble.

At Al Aqsa Hospital it seemed that the patients were taking increasing liberties. They would knock on our accommodation door regularly, at least every ten minutes, day and night, and expect someone to respond. The reasons were varied. Last night, for example, at about 10:30 p.m., there was a knock on the door as a father wanted to show one of the Emergency Medical Team members how successful his son's manual evacuation of the bowel had been. War surgery clearly had challenges.

A major asset to all the work at Al Aqsa Hospital, not just my own, was a visit by the American International Rescue Committee (IRC). I had not expected them but in barely a few hours, the IRC had identified serious shortcomings with infection control. The score used by the IRC for Infection Prevention Control (IPC) allowed a maximum (best) score of 100 per cent. The pass mark was 75 per cent but Al Aqsa Hospital scored 29 per cent. This was far below what it should be, did not surprise me, and went a fair way to explain the hospital's huge infection rate. I talked at length on the drive back to Rafah that evening with the IRC inspectors, who were already formulating plans to improve matters. Not before time in my view.

We had a near miss on the way back to Rafah, by nearly crashing into a tractor and trailer driven by a Palestinian farmer and his local assistant. The loaded trailer was the same width as the single-lane dirt track road, so there was no room for anything except the tractor and trailer. We were travelling in the opposite direction, had several vehicles behind us, and came to a speedy stop nose-to-nose with the Palestinian farmer and his tractor. There was an impasse, he refused to reverse, as did we, so simply glared at each other for at least ten minutes, neither wishing to budge. It was not the best way for a humanitarian organisation to win over the local community, but our reversing would have been a problem as cars were building up behind us.

Eventually the tractor gave way, after much shouting, anger, and Palestinian blaspheming. Throughout the standoff, I was waiting for someone to produce a loaded weapon, but thankfully no one did so. I returned to Rafah unscathed.

Because of the extreme nature of the injuries created by explosions, many of the patients in the hospital had injuries that were complex to handle and it could be debatable to know what to do. One in particular troubled me. It was a 32-year-old woman, yet another innocent civilian injured in an explosion three weeks earlier. This had given her a fracture of her skull, three fractures in her right hand, a laceration to her left face, and a massive fracture of her right shin bone. The shin bone fracture had breached the skin, exposing the broken bone to the air, and was associated with a large loss of bone as well. The force of the explosion had been so large that roughly 15 centimetres of shin bone was missing. The missing bone was likely to be near where she was injured and under the rubble of her house, so unfortunately was impossible to retrieve. I asked several local colleagues what they felt I should do. All manner of ideas were proposed. The first was an amputation but I was reluctant, as was the patient. The problem was that her foot on the fractured side was working well, as was the thighbone above. Consequently, I felt we should do as much as we could to preserve the leg, but that would have meant lots of surgery over many months, maybe years. I estimated at least 20 operations lay ahead of the patient but secretly suspected that was an underestimate. It would take at least 18 months for the patient to heal satisfactorily, even if she healed at all.

The fact was that nothing existed at Al Aqsa Hospital to treat this patient, so all she could do was wait. All I could do was keep her uninfected. Her name was added to the very long list of potential evacuees and it was then a matter of time. A very long time perhaps, during which all manner of other complications might creep in. Bed rest, which was what she was having, could sometimes create more problems than it solved.

War surgery could be extremely difficult, and this patient was an excellent example.

\* \* \*

# Chapter 16

# Spreading the Message

In the early hours of the morning, I had evidence that even the Palestinian doves were tough, which made me feel this war would take a long time to end. I was woken by the loudest of dove coos, barely half a metre from my head. The dove's appearance was followed moments later by a loud crow from Rafah's cockerel. I had left my window slightly ajar for ventilation through the night, and a dove had decided to investigate. It put its head inside the window, clearly saw me, and cooed. I looked at the dove, it stared at me, did not fly away but hopped into the room and walked along the windowsill above my head to take a closer look. After an at least ten-second gaze, it decided I was of no interest, turned, walked back along the windowsill, hopped through the window, and flew away.

I was too dozy to work out what type of dove it was, although I suspect it was a turtle dove. This was thanks to its black tail having a white edge. If I was right, I could expect some affection that day, as that is what a turtle dove symbolises. However, I was astonished at the dove's behaviour, as it had been utterly brazen. There was no chance the same would have happened in the UK. The dove summed up, to me at least, the resilience of the Palestinian nation.

Far in the distance and high in the sky, the *zinnanah* was still buzzing overhead. I noticed that now I talked about "the" *zinnanah* not "a" *zinnanah*, as the buzz was generally continuous. Today it had beaten the cockerel and was making its buzz well before the cockerel had uttered a single squawk.

Paradoxically, I took comfort from the *zinnanah*'s presence, now that I realised it meant I was unlikely to be attacked. My Palestinian colleagues continued to reassure me that I should only worry when the *zinnanah* disappeared, as it was then that the explosions could be expected. The *zinnanah* would subsequently reappear to check the task was done. If anything had been missed, back came the explosions. I am still unsure of the logic of Israeli targeting, judging from the patients I had been seeing in the hospital. There were streams of women, children and the elderly being brought through the front doors. Perhaps the explanation lay in the reported use of AI for target acquisition. When in doubt, it was simpler to blame the computer for its errors as it distanced mankind from the event. I could not see how any human being might justify what I had seen in Palestine. It defied logic that any individual could be so warped.

As I drove northwards along the coast that morning and towards Deir-al-Balah and my work at Al Aqsa Hospital, I saw plenty of local people on the move. It was the turn of those displaced from Gaza City to begin their lengthy walk from Rafah. Those displaced from Khan Yunis had already tried to return but had been beaten back by Israeli missiles and gunfire. I could see those returning to Gaza City were hoping for a better response, but no such luck. They, too, were beaten back, and some were even killed. Plenty were wounded. It appeared that Israel had no intention of allowing them to return. Once again, it seemed there was a land grab underway. As a war surgeon, this meant my work would not be disappearing in a hurry. It had perhaps only just begun.

Last night, near Al Aqsa Hospital, there had been an extensive gunfight between locals and aid delivery trucks. The police had intervened, and there had been plenty of shooting albeit in the air. Gunfire in the urban surroundings of Deir-al-Balah sounded very loud as it echoed off the remaining stone and brick buildings, and within the narrow streets. Fortunately, no one had been killed or wounded. There was an extensive Black Market underway for the control of what aid made it into Gaza, a paltry amount compared with what was waiting to enter from outside and was being prohibited by the Israelis. Nothing entered, and nothing left the territory without Israeli permission. There was always someone able to make money from warfare and the human misery it created.

Aid distribution was a logistic nightmare, as the number of IDP tents became larger by the moment. Meanwhile, some would decide to leave their tent where it was and head off to see if they might retrieve items from their ruined homes or even move back in if the situation allowed. Sadly, so far all attempts at returning had come to nought.

Today was my last day at Al Aqsa before I headed for the UK. What had initially seemed to be a lengthy mission to Gaza, suddenly appeared too short. I was only just beginning to get to grips with the work and yet now my time in the Gaza warzone was coming to an end. That was assuming I could make it through the Rafah crossing, as Israel was thumping war drums noisily, and saying it would assault Rafah irrespective of global opinion.

"You must return to Gaza," I was told by several of my Palestinian colleagues.

"I will if they let me," I replied, realising that Israel knew so much about me that it was up to them if I would ever be permitted to re-enter.

In my mind, I had set aside the day for tidying, packing, and saying farewells, but that was not to be. The moment word spread around the 700 patients, squashed shoulder-to-shoulder in a space for less than one-third that number, that today would be my last at Al Aqsa, patients I had no idea existed materialised as if from nowhere. Mobiles with cracked screens were thrust before me, blood results on crumpled pieces of paper were removed from worn pockets, and unsterile pots of cloudy urine were waved in the air.

"Doctor! What must I do?" asked one Palestinian with a fracture of a bone in his left hand. The injury was three months old, and the man's ring finger barely moved.

"Open and close your hand," I instructed. The man did as I requested but it was clear his ring finger was largely immobile.

"Nothing surgical here," I said. "A hand therapist might achieve something."

"There is none in Gaza. I knew of one, but she has gone missing," said my Palestinian colleague, who was standing alongside me and translating.

"He will have to do the best he can," I said, half smiled at the patient, and gave the tiniest shrug. The man was another example of the long list of patients in Gaza who would benefit from access to proper healthcare, yet circumstance prevented it.

My colleague spoke rapid Arabic, the man nodded and stepped to one side. Behind him was a woman with a painful shoulder, behind her another with a stiff knee, behind her several children, for some reason each with both thighbones broken by an explosion, and behind them another child with a thousand-yard stare. The staring boy, for that was what he was, clearly had major mental problems and needed the expertise and time of a paediatric psychologist. Even then it could take several years for a single case such as the boy's to settle, and occasionally a cure was impossible. In Gaza there was no chance of such treatment becoming available until the fighting stopped and I could see no evidence of that. Israel seemed set on creating mayhem and patients like the ones I had just seen, and the many others around them, would continue their suffering.

## Spreading the Message    161

The throng of people was increasing, with requests for me to see this, that, and everything, so we had to struggle to break through. We did so with difficulty, and I left behind many opinions outstanding as there was simply insufficient time.

Then it was down to the operating theatres and yet another casualty that needed a readjustment of an earlier fixation that had slipped. War surgery is more than about a single operation. It needs the totality of care, from the moment a casualty enters the door, through surgery, onto the ward, and beyond. The real question to ask a war surgeon is not "How many operations did you do?" but "What was the outcome for the patients on whom you operated?" There are many quacks and slashers in war surgery who can appear to be utterly convincing. The real fact to establish is if their patients recover and, if not, why not. There are very few operations in warfare that can settle everything in one go. Al Aqsa Hospital showed this perfectly as there was so much work to do.

I was so occupied with the patients that I almost missed the presentation that had been developed so that the hospital could thank the EMT for all it had done. I made it by a whisker, with seconds to spare. It was held in the Medical Director's office, with Palestinian flags standing proudly at one end. The Medical Director, who had convened the event, was a general surgeon who had been at work since the war began. He was a truly remarkable individual. His speciality was normally bariatric surgery, which is the surgery for obesity. That was in better times. Now, just like me, he had become a war surgeon and had somehow lasted six months of work, with barely any backup, and had still managed to remain in one piece. The room's windows were open, but the floor-length curtains were drawn closed. The presentation began, as was the Arab way, with an obligatory cup of local coffee that gave me a much-needed caffeine fix. I noticed I had begun to flag, had less energy, and was being more easily distracted, so that single tiny cup of coffee did the trick.

The presentation also showed me that nothing escaped the other side's notice. They knew we were there even if no one had officially told them, and they were about to send a warning.

The event had barely begun when there was an enormous, "Thump!" The curtains billowed and my ears rang. Then came another, then another, and finally a fourth. Yet no one even blinked but continued talking as if the enormous noise had never occurred.

"This doesn't worry you, does it?" asked a Palestinian colleague who was sitting beside me.

"Of course not," I lied, while trying to sound convincing. "What was that?" I then asked.

"Let me have a look," said my colleague, got to his feet and peeked around a curtain's edge, looking at the sky. "Ah!" he then declared. "I thought so."

"Please tell me," I asked.

"I can see some falling chaff, or something like it. It will be a countermeasure released by a passing fighter jet."

I nodded my understanding, at least as best I could when my ears were still ringing from four thumps. I tried hard to appear relaxed but was unsure I was succeeding. I looked at the others around me. We formed a group of six and no one was perturbed. Each was talking to the person sat beside them and no one looked concerned at all. We had been subjected to four sonic boom attacks, where a fighter jet breaks the sound barrier directly overhead. These had been used against the Palestinians nearly 20 years previously and had been criticised by the UN at that time. I was surprised the Israelis were still using them but had just become a victim myself. For reference, the meeting was unaffected and proceeded regardless. It was remarkable to see my Palestinian colleagues remain entirely unflapped.

Sonic boom attacks are different to sonic bomb attacks, which I had initially thought might have been the problem. Sonic and ultrasonic weapons (USW) are of various types and use sound to injure or incapacitate an opponent. Some sonic weapons make a focused beam of sound while others produce an area of sound. There is a limited use of sonic weapons now underway. Extremely high-power sound waves can rupture the eardrums of a target and cause severe pain or disorientation. This is usually sufficient to incapacitate a person. Less powerful sound waves can cause humans to experience nausea or discomfort. None of this applied to those of us at the presentation and I made the presumption that because I could still hear, despite distant ringing in my ears, added to the chaff seen by my colleague, we had not been attacked by sonic bombs, only sonic booms. Either way, it made no difference although it was evident we were being sent a message.

The presentation was speedy and involved speeches, a vote of thanks, a certificate to say thank you, and an ongoing invitation to return. My name was misspelt on the certificate, but it made no difference. I needed only to look into the eyes of the staff and patients at Al Aqsa Hospital to know I had been doing the right thing, regardless of the risks I had been taking.

The final day in a location always seems to be a rush, especially when taking photographs. I had much enjoyed a few other occasions in conflict zones when a professional photographer had been on hand. There had been none attached to me during my time in Gaza. Photographs had been difficult throughout my service in the territory, for fear I might be labelled a spy, so many of my images had been taken hurriedly, or snapshots at waist level, and plenty through closed windows. I did find one perfect way of taking photographs without being mistaken for a spy, which was to ask a local to take a photograph for me. They were astonishingly helpful, and the arrangement worked well. I handed my camera to the local, who took the photograph on my behalf and either used my camera from the beginning or sent me a photograph from their own device once done. It worked brilliantly.

The media people also appeared, knowing it was the EMT's final day at Al Aqsa Hospital, and they were keen to film just about everything. Although standing before a camera was something I found instinctively uncomfortable, the media specialists were good at spreading the word – something at which I was completely hopeless – and I felt it was important they said as much as possible.

Much of the Gaza conflict had been associated with a clampdown on reporting, in whatever form that came. Within Israel, the media were mostly publishing the IDF version of events unchallenged and the left-wing newspaper Haaretz had been threatened with financial penalties for sabotaging Israel in wartime. The only permitted trips into Gaza for journalists had been via IDF-controlled embeds. This was where the journalist would travel with the military, so what they would see, or cover would be restricted.

Before leaving the UK, I had also talked with several colleagues working for major news outlets in the land. I had been told they were being restricted in what they could report, and I would have to avoid saying anything political when I returned. There was clearly a major push underway to control how the world saw the conflict in Gaza, and to persuade the globe that one side was right while the other was wrong. Once in Gaza, it was evident that the issue was more complicated, and there was no simple or single solution.

Consequently, when I was asked if I might make a film in the operating theatre after the presentation ceremony was complete, I instantly agreed. Many questions were put to me, in addition to a reminder that I must keep my views apolitical, but I said what I thought, which included the need for equipment improvisation, as Al Aqsa Hospital lacked just about everything. The media folk then vanished, and I had no idea if I had done well, badly, or anything in between. It was then up to them to make what they could of my interview.

Fittingly perhaps, the final patient I saw at Al Aqsa Hospital was a colleague, a consultant who had been caught up in an explosion three months earlier. Explosive injuries are invariably untidy. Skin is shredded and contaminated, not perfectly incised in a clean way. Bone is smashed into small pieces – that is comminuted – not broken tidily with a single transverse fracture. The consultant showed this perfectly, with his entire upper thighbone being smashed into small pieces. He had undergone surgery at the time, and the position of the broken thighbone had been perfectly held in position by the surgeons involved with his care. Sadly, however, there was no sign of the fracture healing. By three months after injury there should have been some evidence of early healing to see on the patient's X-ray, but I could see nothing at all. The problem was what to do?

In the UK I would likely have suggested bone grafting, using bone from the patient's own pelvis. In Gaza it was different. The patient probably had insufficient bone of his own to fill such a large gap anyway, and famine would have run him down, so the bone graft quality would have been poor as well. The operation itself would have taken at least one hour to do, and a wound left open for an hour in a hospital with a near-100 per cent rate of infection was asking for trouble. My solution? Plenty of empathy, a smile, and a handshake. It was better to do nothing and hope. I wished the consultant well and went on my way, while realising what lay ahead of him, a realisation I did not like at all.

Many of the local Palestinians I met asked me to spread the word about their plight when I returned to the UK. They did not feel the world was properly aware of what was happening in Gaza. I could understand why, as there was so much media restriction, with free-thinking limited or even banned. The fact was that the world was fully aware but having difficulty being heard. The Palestinians asked me to do my best to ensure they were heard, and I undertook to do that.

Meanwhile, the war looked to be spreading as Iran had responded to the Damascus attack by launching 300 missiles against Israel. There were no admitted deaths as a consequence, although a 7-year-old girl was reported as being severely injured by missile fragments, some patients sustained minor injuries, and some were treated for anxiety. I am sure that Israel, the USA, and other actors as well had advance notice of the attack. The models of drone used were also largely basic and simple to destroy. Iran suggested that the attack was an end to it. That would depend on Israel, as did so much of the conflict anyway.

\* \* \*

# Chapter 17

# Leaving Gaza

This book was derived from my daily diary, which was initially written in the present tense. I converted the lot into the past tense to make it simpler to read. However, I have made one exception – this chapter. It was written from the heart, on the very morning I departed Gaza, and explained precisely how I was feeling – guilt, exhaustion, and worry. I have left it as it was, completely unedited. Please read it and understand as one day, in that next war zone, wherever it may be, it could be you.

Today I leave Gaza and am full of thoughts. It is presently dark where I am in Rafah, 4:30 a.m., the *zinnanah* is already flying overhead, while in the distance I can hear machine-gun fire and explosions. A friend is playing *Tango to Evora* a couple of metres away as he, too, is a restless sleeper. In Gaza, with conflict all around, the music is almost surreal but utterly delightful, the cockerel is crowing loudly, the dawn chorus has just begun, and the *muazzim* has already made a call to prayer. For a moment, perhaps let down by the distant background noise, I can pretend there is not a war taking place. I can imagine there are not many thousands of dead, dying, disabled, injured, and displaced in my immediate vicinity. That feeling, sadly, lasts for mere moments. I have three hours to get packed and be ready to leave, yet here I am thinking and reflecting. What do I feel?

Guilt for sure. I may have been in Gaza for a shortish time, but I have already created deep friendships, both within my team and the Palestinians we have sought to help. I have given undertakings that I hope I can keep. The woman victim of an opposition missile who determinedly asked me to tell the world what is happening, to spread her message far, and to be sure I tell her case to social media. The man in his sixties with prostate cancer, and who needs lifesaving chemotherapy, yet there is none to be had in Gaza. He is slowly dying as he works his way up an interminable list of patients awaiting evacuation. Or the author of daily war diaries that tell of multiple evacuations from one location to another, loss of family, good friends still buried under rubble, and a vapourised career, who also wishes me to tell the world.

"The Palestinian people need to know they are not alone. Spread their message widely," I am instructed.

Then there is the young surgeon, near fluent in English, manifestly intelligent, who has guided me throughout my time in Gaza. In any other land he would reach the pinnacle of his profession. Yet in Gaza his very existence is uncertain, and that includes his career future.

I feel tired as well, as I may think I have been sleeping but clearly have not. My sleep has been in fits and starts, and I am generally exhausted.

I doze off when I least expect it and find I am walking upstairs one at a time while holding onto the banister. Back home, I would leap up and down, two steps at a time, and think nothing of it. I begin the day tired and end it exhausted, so somehow I need a good sleep.

I feel worried, too, but paradoxically not entirely for myself. The day before I arrived in Gaza seven aid workers were killed by missiles, for no reason other than they were in the wrong place at the wrong time, while the opposition was being self-centred and unthinking. Who knows if it was target acquisition by AI gone wrong, or yet another intentional killing. The stories and the lies will continue, as the first casualty of any war is truth.

Each day I have driven past the spot these fellow humanitarian workers were killed, to reach my hospital, Al Aqsa. The hospital is filled with hardworking professionals, most of whom are unpaid. It would normally house 200 patients, largely maternity. Now it contains at least 700, each injured horribly.

I worry that once I have gone, the opposition will take advantage and assault the hospital, as they have already destroyed most healthcare in Gaza. My hospital was one of the few remaining and even then was barely functioning. The courtyard outside was attacked ten days ago and a *zinnanah* buzzes overhead the hospital continuously, just as it does in Rafah. Less than 24 hours ago, even I was attacked with sonic booms, the windows shaking, the drawn curtains billowing, and my ears still ringing, even now. A friend senses I have been an unwitting human shield while in the hospital, and he may be correct. All I can now do is see if the opposition increases its attacks. I wager it will.

I am worried, too, about those I have left behind in the United Kingdom – family, friends, and colleagues. Some have refused to listen to the news while I have been in Gaza, while others have heard every bulletin. Or, the friend who said before I left, "I am worried about this one," and those with Post-Traumatic Stress Disorder (PTSD) from earlier conflicts whom I have helped treat as I was once military, but whose symptoms have once again been triggered by knowing I am in Gaza.

I am also worried by me, as I know that Gaza has changed me. I am unsure how but those who know me back home will doubtless advise. I will take life easily for a few weeks and allow the Gaza dust to settle. What seems clear is that a great wrong is presently being enacted in Palestine, while the world turns its back and blames anyone other than the side they support. The politicians may spout fine words but to those who have been to Gaza and have directly witnessed the ongoing decimation of Palestinian civilisation – most politicians have not – or to those who have been attacked themselves and watched their lives dissolve, it is evident who is wrong and who is right.

I worry that I will be powerless to change this, that the problem is too massive. Let me return home and try.

\* \* \*

# Acknowledgements

A book such as this would be impossible without the help of so many others, both within and outside Palestine. I am bound to forget someone, so if that someone is you, I beg forgiveness. There is also security to consider as all I need do is mention a name, and a knock on the door, a rustle of a tent flap, perhaps a shell, missile, or gunshot, can be the result. I will thus keep my acknowledgements general, apart from a very few. To all those at Medical Aid for Palestinians (MAP) and the International Rescue Committee (IRC), both within and beyond Gaza, thank you for all you did and continue to do. Each of you is brilliant. For all those at Al Aqsa Hospital in Deir-al-Balah, you are also fantastic. I have no idea how you have done it, but you have. In the middle of this incredible disruption to Palestinian civilisation, you have kept going and continue in this way. Thank you, thank you, thank you. Yet the names I can mention are those of my colleagues who also formed part of this Emergency Medical Team. What a first-class team you have been and may the friendships and trust we have forged between us continue in perpetuity. Thank you for what you have done, are doing, and in some cases will do again when you return. Thanks to each of you – Mahim, Roberto, David, Mohammad, Khaled, and Lukasz. You are amazing. Thank you to Shams Khalil for the extract from their war diary and thank you, too, to the local who accompanied me for most of my time in Gaza. I am keeping you anonymous here, for obvious reasons, but once we have published the data in the scientific literature, data that you will find on these pages, your hard work and professionalism will be clear for all to see. Thank you for looking after me so well and please thank your Mum for the biscuits! It also goes without saying that I owe a massive debt of thanks to my family and friends in the UK. I tried to pretend I was going mountain walking rather than working in Gaza but got the fib wrong. Lying is not my strength. I am grateful for your support throughout. Wonderful and thank you.

\* \* \*

Perhaps I should also acknowledge London's City of Westminster, in addition to England's Dartford Tunnel. I arrived back to the UK from Gaza to find no less than eight parking tickets on my car, which had also been clamped. When I telephoned to say why I had trangressed, and that I had just returned from Gaza, the response was, "They all say that."

Who knows, I suppose they may.

\* \* \*

Dear Reader,

We hope you have enjoyed this book, but why not share your views on social media? You can also follow our pages to see more about our other products: facebook.com/penandswordbooks or follow us on X @penswordbooks

You can also view our products at www.pen-and-sword.co.uk (UK and ROW) or www.penandswordbooks.com (North America).

To keep up to date with our latest releases and online catalogues, please sign up to our newsletter at: www.pen-and-sword.co.uk/newsletter

If you would like a printed catalogue with our latest books, then please email: enquiries@pen-and-sword.co.uk or telephone: 01226 734555 (UK and ROW) or email: uspen-and-sword@casematepublishers.com or telephone: (610) 853-9131 (North America).

We respect your privacy and we will only use personal information to send you information about our products.

Thank you!